MONEY MANAGEMENT WISDOM

8 **$**TEPS TO LIVING *YOUR BEST LIFE*

MERRIE ALLMON ALLEN

MMW
MONEY MANAGEMENT WISDOM

Scripture quotations are from the Life Application Bible, NIV, Tyndale House Publishers, Inc., Wheaton, Illinois, and Zondervan Publishing House, Grand Rapids, Michigan, 2005; MacArthur Study Bible, ESV, John MacArthur, 2016, Crossway Publishing, Wheaton, Illinois, 2016.

Cover Photo by Marlo Laney Photography, Tampa, Florida.

Money Management Wisdom: 8 Steps to Living Your Best Life
Copyright © 2019 By Merrie Allmon Allen
Published by Money Management Wisdom LLC
Tampa, Florida 33578
www.moneymanagementwisdom.net

Library of Congress Control Number: 2019902180
ISBN:978-0-578-40532-2

This book is dedicated to my two beautiful grandsons, Zachariah Christopher Bayard and Elijah Daniel Jackson. I feel abundantly blessed whenever I'm in your presence. Mimi loves you.

Acknowledgements

There are many people who supported me in this project. I'm grateful to my clients, workshop attendees, my team members at Hillsborough County Clerk's Office, and anyone who has ever asked me for advice on personal financial matters. Thank you for sharing your life stories and trusting me for financial guidance.

My family and friends. Thank you for encouraging and supporting me in all my endeavors. I'm especially grateful for my husband, Ricky, for being the most patient person I've ever known. Your love and sacrifice do not go unnoticed.

Yolanda Cook-Killings and Keith Bayard. Thank you for eagerly and diligently reading my manuscript and providing great feedback.

Sam Maxwell, Senior Pastor of the, First Baptist Church of Progress Village; and Pat Frank, Hillsborough County Clerk. I appreciate the opportunity you've given to me to share my knowledge with those under your leadership.

Lastly, I give honor to my Lord and Savior, Jesus Christ, for providing a platform that allows me to use my knowledge, skills, and abilities to do what I love—helping others live their best life.

Table of Contents

Introduction

It's one of the more popular phrases of the day. "I'm living my best life." The proclamation is emblazoned on T-shirts, mugs, and social media memes. Individuals spout the phrase in the most confident manner signifying that all is well, and life is great.

If you dig a little deeper in conversation with these folks, chances are you'll find that most people who claim to be living their best lives are not—especially when it comes to managing their finances. Most people are just trying to make it to the next payday.

- 50% of people live paycheck to paycheck.
- The average credit card debt is $16,245.
- The average student loan debt at $39,400.
- 30% of people over 55 have no retirement savings.

Given these statistics, it's safe to assume that many people are experiencing some measure of money-related stress. When people are under stress, they are less effective in their tasks and far from living their best lives.

One reason people face financial challenges is because they haven't learned how to manage money. Most high school curriculums do not include personal finance. In the 17 states that do, the course is not a requirement for high school graduation. This lack of education has caused people to make poor financial decisions in their teen and young adult life that yield adverse consequences. Sometimes the effects of those decisions play well into adulthood. The Bible tells us that we are destroyed from lack of knowledge.[1]

I wrote *Money Management Wisdom—8 Steps to Living Your Best Life* to educate and inspire you to manage your money in a manner that allows you to have the best possible life in every area that matters. My goal is to help you gain a new perspective, understand a new purpose, yield to your calling, and create a new plan for your money. I want to help you begin to think differently about money and gain the power to stay in control of your finances.

Living your best life may be pursuing education, a career, or fame and fortune. It may be finding that perfect companion and creating the family you've always wanted. It may be enjoying the fruits of your labor by traveling the world. Or perhaps it's the grit and grind of running your own business. You may think you're living your best life by becoming involved in community or church activities. Maybe enjoying the social life or networking with others to make things happen is your thing. Whatever actions or experiences constitute living your best life, there's a good chance that money is involved in some fashion. When you are not behaving properly with your money, you may not be able to participate in your best life activities or realize your best-life dreams without going further into debt.

Your journey to living your best financial life must begin with a conscious decision and a willingness to change the way you think about money. For many people, money is thought of as a tool to get the things they need. In many cases, the focus is more on getting things they want. This is where most people get in trouble. You view money today in much the same way people viewed sex and drugs in the 1960s—a free for all. If it feels good, do it. No holds barred. In the same manner, money is used to get what you want at any cost without restrictions or boundaries. If you want it, get it. This kind of thinking has led many into what seems like unsurmountable debt; so much that people are becoming depressed and sick from financial stress. This is certainly not living your best life.

If you think money's sole purpose is to allow you to buy whatever you want, as much as you want, and as quickly as you can get it, your behavior is going to align with your thoughts. You may pursue money by any means necessary with no regard as to how it may be affecting your relationships, health, or spiritual life. The fact is, money *is* a tool, but it's a tool that is meant to be used not only for yourself but also for the benefit of others.

In his teaching to new Christians, Apostle Paul instructed them to stop behaving like everyone else and to change their behavior by "transforming" their mind.[2] If you've been facing financial challenges, struggling to get a handle on your finances, stressed out due to overwhelming debt, or all of the above, you can change the behavior that caused you to be in your current situation if you're willing to change your thoughts and attitude and start seeing things from a new perspective.

Money Management Wisdom: 8 Steps to Living Your Best Life encourages you to view money as a tool to be used in conjunction with your life's calling. In doing so, you will experience the real power of money. Your money will have the power to change your life as well as the lives of those who cross your path.

This book will help you understand why you're here. You're not here to be consumed with debt and other financial problems. Your purpose is not to spend your precious years climbing out of debt. You have a special and specific calling on your life, and when you are walking in that calling you will undoubtedly be living your best life. You will learn the meaning of stewardship and understand the role it plays in managing your money.

You'll learn to identify the barriers that keep you from living the life God intended for you. I'll teach you the ins and outs of credit and debt and help you create a plan to reach your financial goals. Lastly, you'll learn how to practice contentment and generosity to experience maximum fulfillment.

As you walk through these steps on your journey to living your best life, there is one thing you absolutely must carry with you. You cannot possibly live your best life without wisdom. Proverbs 4:7

says, "Wisdom is the principle thing; therefore, get wisdom." When you walk with wisdom, you'll be protected from foolishness and you'll make better decisions. Being able to make wise decisions will be a game changer.

John Piper defines wisdom as having factual knowledge, situational insight, and the necessary resolve to accomplish a goal. When it comes to seeking direction or making decisions, financial or otherwise, wisdom dictates that you gain knowledge. Do your research. You must also possess insight into the situation. Insight may come from past experiences, consulting with others who have "been there," and biblical guidance. What does your gut tell you? The final leg of wisdom is to be ready to make a decision. When you combine knowledge, situational insight, and resolve, you'll have the highest likelihood of success in making good decisions and achieving your desired outcome.

Change can sometimes be a scary thing. However, you cannot continue managing your money the same way and expect different results. The fact that you picked up this book tells me that you're ready to do something new. If you take these eight steps to heart, you will change your life and make it count for something far beyond what you can ever imagine. Take a leap of faith and jump right into it. I promise you'll have a soft landing. Here's to you living your best life ever!

Step 1 - Know Your Role

For we are God's workmanship, created in Christ Jesus to do good works, which God prepared in advance for us to do.   *(Ephesians 2:10)*

An important aspect of living your best life is operating within the space that God ordained just for you. You can walk through life engaged in many things—careers, hobbies, club memberships, etc., and you may serve many roles. However, the best of you and the best of what you have to offer the world will be exemplified when you are fulfilling the role designed just for you.

We often hear of people who are searching for their purpose in life. There are tons of books written to help people "figure out" what they're supposed to be doing. We're convinced that there's some great big mystery about our life that we have yet to discover, so we go through life searching for the great unknown—sometimes for years. I don't believe God sends us on a scavenger hunt to find our life's calling. That's not to say that He won't grow us through some experiences that help us identify our calling and equip us to serve others better. My point is that we should not struggle and stress over trying to figure out what God wants us to do. We also should not be still and do nothing while we're waiting.

Let me explain what I mean when I use the word "calling." You often hear the word "purpose" being used to describe one's unique role in the world. I want to make the distinction between the concepts of purpose and calling. According to King Solomon, we all have one common purpose.[3] After he'd seen all, done all, and acquired all the material things he could ever want, King Solomon concluded that the whole matter or purpose in life for mankind is to honor and obey God. This is our *purpose*. Our calling is the unique role we play in serving others to fulfill our purpose of glorifying God. He created us to do good works—works that He prepared for us in advance.[4] How exciting to know that it was decided before we were yet born what our life assignment would be.

Author and life coach Valorie Burton said it like this: "*Your purpose (calling) is about making a difference in the lives of others. You cannot live your life's purpose(calling) unless you are in some way serving others. How is someone's life better because they crossed your path?* [5]

The best way to discover your calling is to be intentional about serving others. Live your life, go to work, run your business, serve in church, coach your kid's ballgame, attend your sorority or fraternity events, volunteer in the community, or do whatever it is that you do in life. Wherever you go and whatever you do in life, look for those opportunities to serve others.

Use the talents that have been gifted to you by the creator to help others. You may be good at organizing, administering, coaching, mentoring, financial planning, public speaking, etc. As you do these things, be mindful of your purpose. Even if you have not discovered your distinct calling, you can always live up to your purpose in the *way* that you do things. When you intentionally engage others and make yourself available while displaying kindness, compassion, and love—attributes of God, you won't have to look for your calling, your calling will find you.

I have always loved working with young people and found myself drawn to activities that placed me in the role of teaching and mentoring. When I was in the Navy, I supervised younger sailors. My service in the church always involved young people. On my job, 50% of my staff is made up of young adults. Having a penchant for managing money and coaching young people, it wasn't extremely hard for my calling to find me. I fulfill my purpose (obeying and glorifying God) through my calling to educate and inspire individuals to live their best lives through the proper management of their money using Godly principles.

Your calling may be running a business, public speaking, playing sports, teaching, singing, dancing, nursing, or being a mom.

You may be wondering how your calling is unique if others are doing the same thing. While it's true that there are plenty of teachers, nurses, and business owners, there's only one you. God made you special and gave you a unique personality. You have special attributes and abilities. When you combine your unique characteristics with ordained skills, wisdom, passion, and commitment, you will be the one person who can reach and connect with others in such a way that their lives are significantly impacted.

What does money management have to do with your calling and your purpose? As you are living out your calling, you want to do so unencumbered. You don't want unnecessary burdens weighing you down, particularly burdens resulting from the mismanagement of money. Once you understand why you're here, your financial goals and decisions should align with your calling to ultimately help you achieve your purpose. Our money is limited. When you know what God wants you to do in life, you can focus your money and time in that direction. Knowing your reason for being will streamline your life and keep you from spending money frivolously on things that don't fit in with your mission.

One of the leading causes of stress is worries over money. If you're facing serious money problems, so much that you can't pay bills or debt collectors are calling, chances are you are experiencing some level of stress. Over a sustained period, stress can cause health issues, such as migraines, heart disease, and a reduced immune system making you vulnerable to infections.

When you are stressed or sick, your calling may be hindered. You may be excited and passionate about your unique role in life. However, if you're not healthy, you can't be fully present. For example, if your calling is to teach and you frequently call out sick, this affects your students and others who have to cover for you. If you're running a business and you're not able to make your calls and appointments or service your customers, your business is going to suffer. Who gets the glory out of that? Remember—only you can do what you're called to do in the way you're called to do it. When you are not present physically or mentally, something is missing. You bring a uniqueness to your calling. Whether you're running a business, teaching, or mentoring, you can't *give* your best when you're not *at* your best.

Money woes may also hinder your calling by preventing you from contributing financially towards your efforts. Just because God gives you a calling doesn't mean that He doesn't intend for you to use your resources. If you work with kids, you may have to sponsor some excursions from time to time. My calling at one point in my life was serving as the ministry leader for middle-school praise dancers. Because of church budgeting challenges, there were many times I was able to fund the girls' dancewear and props. I found immense joy in being able to do that. I never requested reimbursement for the expenses because I felt I was taking ownership of my calling, and I was blessed financially to be able to do it. In turn, I was blessed *because* of it. Ultimately, God got the glory. Had I been a poor manager of my money, I would not have had that experience.

Now, let me just say this about the importance of identifying your calling. When I say that you should try to be involved in different things and look for opportunities to serve others, I don't mean that you should make a lifelong habit of running from one endeavor to the other with no defined direction or purpose. You should be intentional in your efforts to serve others and have your eyes and heart open to meaningful opportunities.

Too often, people move halfheartedly from one thing to the other involving themselves in multiple ventures simultaneously. Yet, they're not able to give 100% to any one of them. They may be involved in every community event or take advantage of every volunteer opportunity. Or, they may look for something big and prominent to claim as their life's calling. Not all callings require an audience. Some callings are small and require you to be in the background. Whether big or small, all roles are significant and valuable in God's sight.

If you're not intentional and focused, you will end up being busy and spending a lot of money and time with nothing to show for your efforts. You may sacrifice time with your family, and your relationships may begin to suffer. We can do a lot of things, but it's difficult to simultaneously do a lot of things with excellence. Find one or two things that you do well and put your unique stamp on it. Continue to build on that until you are performing at your best in that role. Channel your efforts and prioritize your spending so that you are making the most of your time and your money as you align them with your unique gifts of service. Your gifts (calling) will make room for you and give you the platform from which you can shine brightest for His glory. Then, you will truly be living your best life.

Step 1 - Know Your Role

Step 2 - Practice Good Stewardship

The earth is the Lord's and everything in it, the world, and all who live in it.

(Psalms 24:1)

Nothing you have belongs to you. Even when you've paid off everything you purchased, those things still don't belong to you. This means your car, home, clothing, and bank account are not yours to do with what you will. You're probably wondering what the heck I'm saying. After all, you're the one who gets up each day and go to work. You're the one who saved the money that's in your bank account. You're the one making the payments on your car and home. What do I mean it's not yours? Well, it's time you know the truth. Everything you have belongs to God.[6]

We are convinced that we own our "stuff," and we claim it with an attitude of entitlement. Accepting that God is the true owner requires you to adopt a new mindset. You've been given the fortitude to acquire those things. You have also been granted the authority and privilege to manage *your* stuff. However, we are not owners and we are not entitled. We are appointed stewards or managers over all that has been "loaned" to us.

There is a significant difference in being a steward and being an owner, and it's important that you have a firm understanding of that difference. How you view yourself in this regard will have an impact on the decisions you make for your life and your money.

An owner has the right to use his time, gifts or talents, and resources as he wishes. He has no obligation to answer to anyone and is usually the final decision maker in all matters related to his stuff.

The ownership mentality becomes evident in the way some individuals behave including how they treat their bodies. They practice unhealthy habits, such as drug use, poor food choices, a sedentary lifestyle, and generally not taking care of themselves. Living an unhealthy lifestyle will not allow you to live your best life for yourself or others.

Understanding that your body is a gift from God and that it should be used for a greater purpose should make you more conscious of how you treat yourself. If you have a spouse or children, you are accountable to them for how you take care of yourself. Staying healthy will ensure that you are available for your family members.

Having an owner mentality also causes people to misuse their money. I was standing in line at my local convenience store. There was a woman in front of me being waited on, and the cashier was taking an unusually long time. I'm patiently waiting to pay for my Coke Zero (don't judge me). Finally, the lady finishes her transaction, and as she turns to leave, she struggles to fit what must have been at least 200 scratch-off lottery tickets into her purse. I'm standing there dumbfounded with my mouth wide open. All I could think about is what I could have done with the amount of money she spent to purchase those tickets. I don't want to sound judgmental because I don't know her situation. She may have been buying tickets for an office pool. However, this is what I know: when you are living your best life by properly allocating your monetary resources, you won't waste your money relying on chanceless gambles to meet your needs.

If you're in debt or otherwise struggling in your finances, chances are you're not effectively managing your money. Living your best life includes setting proper spending priorities. Trust God to meet your needs, not the state lottery system that intentionally stacks the odds against you.

I know a family who inherited a home from their parents. One of the family members lives in the house and is constantly negotiating foreclosure proceedings with the bank. Yet, the relative is known to spend upwards of $500 each month on lottery tickets.

Clearly, this behavior displays a blatant mismanagement of resources provided that were intended to meet the family member's need of shelter. We should trust the promises of God that tell us He will provide our needs.[7] He provides the resources—what we choose to do with them is on us. When we purposely misappropriate resources, we should be prepared to deal with the consequences.

The steward mentality recognizes God as the owner of everything and believes that He loans things to individuals to serve as managers. The expectation is that the recipient will take care of what they're given, increase its value, and use it to be an influencer in service to others while sharing His goodness.

A steward is accountable for how well they manage what is entrusted to them. Once you prove yourself to be faithful over a few things, God will trust you with more.[8] Think about it. If you buy your child a bike and they don't take care of it, destroying it in a matter of weeks, are you inclined to say yes when they ask you for a better bike? If you run a business and you're not taking care of your customers properly, can you expect that your business will gain more customers? There's no difference than when you mismanage the things God gives you. How can you expect to get more if you don't take care of what you have?

The Bible tells the story of a man who was going on a trip. He left his servants behind with an assignment to manage his money. He gave each of the three servants a portion of his wealth *according to what each could handle* so there would be no excuses. The first two servants invested and doubled the money given to them. The third servant dug a hole in the ground and hid the money, which was a customary practice for those who wanted to safeguard their valuables. When the master returned, he was pleased with the first two servants' management of his money. Even though the servants received different amounts, each of them doubled what they'd received. And because they each did what was expected, they received the same reward. As the master approached the third servant, the servant began to offer excuses for why he had not done well with the money he received. The servant claimed he felt the master was too hard on people, so he hid the money (out of fear of losing it). The master chastised the servant telling him that at the very least, he could have put the money in the bank to gain interest. The "lazy" servant had not even done that. The master took the money from the lazy, fearful servant, leaving him with nothing, and gave it to the servant who had the most money.

This story shows that it doesn't matter if you have a little or a lot, whether you drive a Benz or a Prius, whether you live in a house on the hill or in a bungalow in the valley, everyone is expected to manage what's been given to them and to make the most of it.

If you do your job well, you will be rewarded. If you don't do well, even what you have will be taken.[9] How might your resources be taken? Making unwise decisions is a sure way to have your money taken away. When you are paying interest because you carry a balance on your credit card each month, your money is being taken away. When you're paying late fees because you failed to pay your bills on time, your money is being taken away. When you've gotten yourself in a debt situation and can't pay your mortgage and you're facing foreclosure, your home may be taken away. When you regularly and substantially "invest" in the lottery, your money is being taken away. When you don't save or invest, you may forfeit your kids' college or your worry-free retirement. These are just some examples of the consequences of not being a good steward.

To live your best life, you must acknowledge where your resources come from and manage them well so that your actions gain the attention of others—not for the purpose of bragging, but for the opportunity to pay homage to the giver.

Some signs that you may NOT be practicing good stewardship are: [10]

- You spend money buying things to keep up with others.
- You spend money to buy things that make you feel important (from God's view, you're already important).
- You borrow money (to include using credit cards) to purchase things that depreciate or have no future value, such as cars, clothing, food.
- You spend money to indulge an obsession or addiction (shopping, gambling, excessive entertainment, drugs/alcohol).
- You neglect to pay your debts and bills on time.
- You pursue wealth through get-rich-quick schemes.
- You spend money to buy love and affection (people should love you for who you are, not for the material things you provide.
- You don't save or invest for future needs.
- You don't have a formal plan (budget) to help you monitor your spending and help you reach your financial goals.

If your behavior mirrors any action from this list, you are at a crossroads. You get to choose which direction you want to go. You can continue down the road of selfish and meaningless spending, or you can pivot and take the first step towards managing your money from a stewardship perspective.

Step 2 - Practice Good Stewardship

Step 3 - Avoid Barriers

Like a city whose walls are broken down is a man who lacks self-control.

(Proverbs 25:28)

When you decide to make major changes in your life, such as losing weight, starting a business, continuing your education, or changing your spending habits, you will face challenges. When it comes to financial challenges, you must identify and avoid barriers that block you from moving towards your financial goals.

Four barriers prevent you from advancing to a healthy financial future:

1. Lack of self-control
2. Lack of discipline
3. Procrastination
4. Comparative influence

While struggling through the effects of poor money habits, many of you manage to live in a "quiet" state of stress and discontentment while displaying a public persona that indicates life is great when in fact, it is not. Not being able to navigate or avoid these barriers contribute to uncontrolled spending, which leads to credit use, which leads to debt, which can lead to relationship and job problems. Ultimately, the consequences may lead you into a spirit of despair and eventually depression. Understanding how these barriers interfere with your efforts to reach your goals will prevent you from falling into their trap.

Lack of Self-control

Self-control is the inability to exercise restraint over your impulses, emotions, or desires.[11] Lacking this critical life skill will affect your finances and every area of your life. Self-control is so important that it is a benchmark for elementary school students. Behavioral professionals understand that the earlier one learns to master himself, the better chance they'll have leading productive lives. The kid who learns to wait his turn when playing a game and raise his hand in class before speaking is learning patience and how to delay gratification.

Walter Mischell, a Stanford University professor, conducted a study in the '60s and '70s called The Marshmallow Experiment. In this experiment, children between the ages of four and six were told they could have one marshmallow now or two marshmallows in 15 minutes. Only 30 % of the children chose to wait for the chance to have two marshmallows. The follow-up on these children revealed that those who were able to practice self-control and delay gratification had fewer behavior problems, were more popular with their peers, and sustained friendships. They also scored higher on their SATs. The higher scores may be contributed to their ability to exercise critical thinking and problem-solving. Self-control also contributes to kids' ability to resist peer pressure.[12]

The Bible is clear on the importance of self-control and lists it as a character trait necessary for a healthy and successful life.[13]

So, what does it look like for those adults struggling with self-control? Many relationships are destroyed for lack of self-control. During contentious moments of conflict, people tend to submit to their impulses and emotions and display behavior or say things they later regret. Perhaps you can think of a time when you "went off" on someone because they said or did something that rubbed you the wrong way. Instead of taking a step back to consider the situation or the challenges the other person might be facing, you just went right into a verbal offence. After taking some time to assess the situation, or after reaping the consequences of your actions, you regretted the encounter. Sound familiar? In a situation like this, it's best to withdraw, delay your need to get revenge or "handle it" and think about how the response you choose will contribute to the best possible outcome.

Financially, lack of self-control or the inability to delay gratification can derail your financial plans. How many times have you gone to the grocery store to buy milk and bread and end up leaving with $50 worth of food? Who can resist the buy-one-get-one deals? On the surface, these impulse purchases may seem harmless. However, when you begin to track your spending, you'll be astounded by how much they impact your bottom line.

Lack of self-control is seen in the couple who decides to take a Sunday drive and stops at a car dealership just to "look." The salesman convinces them to test drive one of the cars, and the next thing you know the couple is driving away in a brand-new vehicle—a significant purchase that was not part of their financial plan.

The stakes were a little higher in the case of Sheree (not her real name). Sheree desperately wanted to purchase a home. She began putting her plan together and started looking at model homes and gathering decorating ideas. Knowing that Sheree was not in a good financial place, I questioned her readiness to purchase a home. After a lengthy conversation, I convinced her to wait two years which would give her time to save for a nice down payment. She agreed that was a good plan.

One day, Sheree and I were hanging out, and we drove past a new home development. As I expected, Sheree wanted to look at the model homes. I hesitantly agreed knowing this was probably not a good idea. To make a long story short, of the four models we looked at, the very last one, according to Sheree, was her dream home and perfectly suitable for her. "It must be a sign," she said. The location was perfect, the size was perfect, the layout was perfect, everything was perfect—except she couldn't afford it. The price was significantly above her budget.

Sheree decided to borrow the remainder of the down payment from her employer-sponsored retirement fund. Unfortunately, a year later her company downsized, and her position was eliminated. As a result, the money she borrowed from her 401(k) became due in 90 days. She was not able to repay the loan in the time allowed, so it was considered an early distribution and taxed as regular income. She was also penalized 10% for early withdrawal. Sheree was forced to sell the house at a loss. Sadly, she had no emergency fund to fall back on.

The lesson learned here is that practicing self-control can save you a world of heartache and headache. Sheree was on the right track and made the right decision to delay her home purchase. However, once the shiny object was thrown at her, she let her emotions and impulsiveness take over rational thinking.

Once you decide on a financial plan, stick with it. Don't allow yourself to become sidetracked. If you've made your decision based on a well-thought plan and you're fully aware of the facts and consequences, you cannot allow impulse and emotion to take over. Exercise self-control and know that you'll have a better outcome if you're patient. Remember the marshmallows. Better things come to those who live their best life by practicing self-control and delaying gratification.

Lack of Discipline

Discipline is often confused with self-control. Webster defines discipline as training that corrects, molds, or perfects the mental faculties or moral character.[14] While self-control is the *short-term* ability to restrain yourself when faced with choices that may result in negative consequences, discipline is the ability to restrain yourself *over an extended time* (long-term) from choices that may result in negative consequences. The more you practice self-control, the more disciplined you become.

For example, you've decided to live a healthier lifestyle that includes making better food choices and getting more exercise. Self-control is showing restraint when dining out and not ordering dessert. Discipline comes into play when you've decided to forego sweets or junk food altogether. You start out *practicing* self-control. Through consistent and committed behavioral changes, you become disciplined. Perhaps one of your decisions would be to wake up a half an hour earlier to exercise. Self-control would be getting out of bed (kill the impulse to sleep in) and making your way to the treadmill. You become disciplined by being consistent. Before long, your morning workout becomes a habit and a regular part of your morning routine. The results? A healthier you!

Financially, you cannot get ahead or be successful with a financial plan if you're not disciplined. Whether it's saving and investing, working on a debt elimination plan, or budgeting, if you operate with a hit-or-miss mentality, you will not get the results you desire. If you're running a business, you can't show up *sometimes* and *you* can't advertise *sometimes*. Likewise, when working toward a better financial future, you can't save money sometimes and you can't monitor your spending sometimes. To bring about meaningful change, you must become disciplined by consistently taking actions that better your financial situation.

When it comes to saving and investing, once you decide to start, you must exercise restraint from activities that cause you to spend frivolously and excessively. I often hear people complain because they're not able to save. Again, most people do not have the money saved to cover an emergency, much less to apply towards investing. Unfortunately, many people do not make spending decisions based on their future needs. They make decisions based on what they can enjoy now. In many cases, those same individuals who complain about not having any money saved place their priorities on weekly shopping trips, happy hours, vacations, new cars, etc.

Those who are most successful in meeting their financial goals are disciplined. They consistently contribute to their financial future. They have learned to practice delayed gratification. That's not to say that you cannot enjoy life while preparing for your future. You can do both. The problem is when you've misplaced your priorities and are so busy living your best life spending, shopping and partying, that you ignore the concepts of sacrifice, moderation, and preparation for future life events.

Procrastination
We've all been there. We put off dreaded tasks that we don't want to deal with. The dictionary definition of procrastination is to put off something intentionally and habitually that should be done.[15] The word to focus on is *habitually*. When procrastination becomes habitual, it can seriously affect your relationships, work, health, spiritual life, and finances.

Your boss may look past one or two missed deadlines, but a habitual practice of missing deadlines is likely to result in disciplinary action or even termination. You put off going to the doctor for routine visits and now you have full-blown diabetes or heart disease—conditions that may have been preventable with early intervention. Your homeowner's or car insurance policy expires, and you've procrastinated in getting them renewed. You have a car accident or your roof collapses, and you must now come out of your pocket to pay for repairs. You ignore the bills staring at you from the table, hoping they will somehow pay themselves, or better yet, disappear. You pay the bills late and incur late charges. You're interested in being promoted at work. The job posted last week and you've yet to get your resume together. Before you know it, the deadline passes, and you never got around to submitting your application. A business colleague tells you to call her next week about a business opportunity. You call two weeks later, and the opportunity was given to someone else.

Here's the thing with procrastination; it will always cost you more than you're willing to pay. Whether it costs you money or missed opportunities—it will always cost you something. How many times have you made a new year resolution to get your finances in order? Every year that you procrastinate and put off making the necessary changes, it's costing you more in credit card interest, lost investment growth, financial protection of an emergency fund, growing debt, etc.

Why do you procrastinate if you know it will result in negative consequences? There may be six reasons you allow procrastination to stop you from living your best life:[16]

1. You don't realize just how short life really is. Think about this—if you're 40 years old, statistically speaking, you've already spent 50% of your allotted years.[17] Get stuff done! Fix your money. Pursue that dream.

2. You're a perfectionist. Stop waiting for perfect timing or perfect conditions to do what you must do. Don't wait until you have more money to begin saving. Don't wait until you get your tax refund to pay off your credit cards. Start paying a little extra and be consistent. When it comes to projects or assignments, there is nothing wrong with wanting to do your best. The problem is that you spend so much time analyzing or perfecting a process that you never complete it. Dave Ramsey, a well-known personal finance guru, calls this "paralysis of analysis." King Solomon, the wisest man who ever lived, warns about over contemplating. If you spend so much time watching and waiting, you won't reap the benefits of productivity.[18] You've got to get your head out of the cloud and make things happen. Or, as my wise mother used to say to me, "You've got to either pee or get off the pot!"

3. Fear of failure. Perhaps the reason you never get around to accomplishing tasks, creating and following a budget, or pursuing your dreams is that you've convinced yourself that you won't succeed. No one succeeds in everything all the time, and those who have any measure of success have had their share of failures. What's the worst that could happen? It won't be the end of the world. Failure simply means you had an opportunity to learn what doesn't work.

4. Lack of goals. You may procrastinate because you don't have any goals. If you don't know where you're going, then you're certainly in no hurry to get there. You may have goals or things you want to accomplish, but they're stuck in your head. The problem is that you haven't written them down and created a plan to reach them. What's your plan? What's your timeline? If one of your goals is to become debt free, how do you propose to accomplish that goal? Increase your income, decrease your spending, or both. What sacrifices are you willing to make? When identifying, setting, and meeting goals, you can't just talk the talk. You've got to act.

5. You're overwhelmed. Procrastination can be a side effect of having too much going on in your life. Having multiple projects and tasks makes it difficult to decide which ones to complete first. You owe e-mails, and phone calls to numerous people. You promised to be on the anniversary committee at church. It's your turn to get goodies for your kid's class. You must order inventory for your business, and your spouse is pouting because the romance has been slim. It's just too much. So, what do you do? Nothing.

6. You're just plain lazy. Ouch! This is the scariest reason of all for procrastinating. Granted, we all have our moments of laziness or those days when we just don't feel like doing anything. However, some people find themselves practicing laziness regularly. They do not attempt to have a productive life or complete any tasks for themselves or anyone else. Others tend to write them off or not be bothered with them because lazy people are not dependable. Lazy people do not display any ambition and are likely to miss out on many of life's opportunities. The Bible warns about laziness and tells us that lazy people want much and get little, but it's the one who works hard who prospers.[19] Be careful though, if you or someone you know exhibit behaviors typically associated with severe laziness, consider that it may be a sign of depression.

What can you do to get around the barrier of procrastination? I've listed some tips below that work for me. I suggest completing this exercise weekly. You may need to tweak it during the week due to changing deadlines. The key to successfully getting things done is to review your task list frequently:

- Identify the important things in your life and list them in priority order. Perhaps those things are faith, family, and your vocation.
- Identify pending tasks related to those things you identified as being important and enter the due date for each task.
- Focus on activities necessary to complete the most important task (in due date order). Completing smaller steps of the task each day may motivate you to move forward.
- If you fail to accomplish a task for one week, roll the task to the list for the following week.
- Discipline yourself to remain focused.
- Treat yourself to a small reward once you complete a task. For example, I record my favorite shows and watch them on the weekends. I've disciplined myself not to indulge until I've met my goals for the week. Practicing delayed gratification by creating an incentive and reward system will keep you from becoming sidetracked and decrease procrastination.
- Accept that you can't say "yes" to every request for your time. "No" is a complete sentence and you don't need an explanation.

Comparative Influences

The last barrier to living your best life is the practice of comparing yourself with others. Even though we pride ourselves on being our own persons, we can be heavily influenced by our peers, and we often measure our progress or success based on what someone else has accomplished. Marketing experts have mastered the practice of making people feel as if they lack something if they don't own a certain product. Ford commercials asks the question, "Have you driven a Ford lately?" The commercial implies that if you have not driven a Ford lately, you are missing out on something big. L'Oréal cosmetic brand advertising tagline says, "L'Oréal— Because *I'm* worth it." The implication is that you can't possibly value yourself unless you use their product.

Comparing what you have to others and longing to have the same things can take you out of your financial lane and cause you to go into debt trying to keep up. Keeping up with the Jones' is still alive for many and is even more prevalent with the popularity of social media.

One of the biggest forums where comparative influence thrives is social media, which I've dubbed the modern-day version of Show & Tell. There have been multiple studies on social media's influence on one's self-esteem or how individuals see themselves and measure their worth. Many people compare their lives to those staged on social media. Someone who is insecure may feel even more so from constantly scrolling and seeing a multitude of selfies taken with the beauty enhancer feature on smartphone cameras.

I recently hired a photographer to take marketing photos of me. The photo shoot included a makeup session. As I was explaining my make-up color options to the artist, I decided it was better to show her a picture of how I usually wear my makeup to give her a reference point. When I showed her the photo on my phone, she was visibly relieved. She told me that she was glad that I had not shown her one of those beautified filtered photos. Apparently, she gets a lot of requests from women asking her to make them look like their selfie. She said that she doesn't have the heart to tell them that makeup can only do so much towards making their face slim, eyes big, nose smaller and lips bigger!

My point is this: don't believe everything you see on social media. Lavish vacations, exquisite meals, new homes, and new cars are all nice for those who can afford them. Don't envy or become jealous of what someone else has. Every lifestyle choice has a price. Many people who appear to be living the baller lifestyle are carrying deep debt to maintain that lifestyle. They are paying a high price to buy an image because their self-worth is tied to their possessions. They are living what they *believe* to be their best life. The Bible calls these people out, saying there are those who pretend to be rich, but they have nothing, and there are others who pretend to be poor and yet has great wealth.[20] This is evident when we see millionaires driving regular inexpensive cars and dressing in jeans and T-shirts. The millionaires who clearly can afford luxury cars and designer clothing don't feel the need to "prove" their fiscal worth. But then we see individuals who can't afford the luxury vehicles and designer clothing, indulging themselves—pretending to be rich.

Remember Sheree and the premature home purchase? Well, let me give you the back story. A mutual acquaintance of ours had recently purchased a beautiful home. Sheree was seemingly obsessed over the fact that this woman was able to purchase a home in a very up and coming neighborhood. Sheree made much more money than this woman, and she wondered how the woman was able to afford such a home. Sheree would drive through the woman's neighborhood periodically to view the house being built. I later learned that Sheree visited the builder's office to inquire on the price of the woman's home.

In the pursuit of her home, Sheree's decision to leave her financial lane was driven by jealousy. She kept her eyes on what someone else was doing and reasoned that she was entitled to the same. Perhaps the woman Sheree was imitating received an inheritance, or she may have been saving money through the years to purchase her home. She may have put herself in a debt situation she'll later regret. The point is that we don't know the sacrifices people make or the circumstances by which they acquire their possessions. Therefore, we shouldn't be jealous or envious, and we certainly shouldn't try to keep up. Stay in your financial lane.

When you compare yourself to others or focus on what they have, you rob yourself of happiness and contentment, and you begin focusing on what you don't have. God's blessings no longer seem sufficient. You must know that you are enough all by yourself. An abundance of possessions means nothing. Possessions don't make you a better person. You are enough because you were fearfully and wonderfully made by God—the ultimate designer. And His works are wonderful.[21]

Learning self-control and discipline and avoiding procrastination and comparative influences will have you well on your way to living your best life.

Step 3 - Avoid Barriers

Step 4 - Avoid the Credit and Debt Trap

The rich rule over the poor, and the borrower is servant to the lender. (Proverbs 22:7)

The numbers tell the story. Households that carry debt balances have an average of $15,654 in credit card debt and pay an average of $904 in interest annually.[22] This is just credit card debt. When you consider other debt, such as home mortgage, student loan, and automobile debt, the picture is even bleaker. We've become accustomed to using credit in all its forms, and as a result, we've accumulated ungodly amounts of debt. Sadly, many of us are conditioned to think this is normal—that it's the American way and a by-product of living in a free capitalistic society where anyone can make a buck at the expense of another. The banking industry has taken full advantage of consumerism, making over $104 billion in credit card interest and fees over the past year.[23]

Simply put, using credit in any capacity means that you are taking out a loan and incurring debt. The mere fact that you use credit is evidence that you probably can't afford to purchase many of the things you buy. Just because you're able to make the monthly payments doesn't mean you can afford the purchase. How do you know if you can afford something? If you can pay cash for it and the purchase does not interfere with other financial obligations and goals, you can probably afford it

If you have goals with higher priorities, such as paying down debt, saving your emergency fund, or contributing towards college and retirement, you can't afford to overindulge in "stuff." For example: If your goal is to contribute to your child's college fund and you are not able to do so because your credit card bills are consuming your income, then you can't afford to buy the jewelry, vacation, hair, sneakers, etc. You would be choosing stuff over your kid's education.

Many of you use credit cards as a convenience for reserving hotels and rental cars or to accumulate reward points. That's great if you're disciplined to pay your balance on time each month to avoid late fees and interest. The problem is that most people are not disciplined to limit their credit card use to transactions of convenience or reward-earning purchases. Studies show that 36% of reward cardholders don't understand their rewards programs and worse, only 25% of cardholders redeem their monthly rewards.[24]

Most people struggle with debt because they've chosen to live a lifestyle that is not commensurate with their level of income. Credit allows you to buy the lifestyle you want, as opposed to living the lifestyle you can afford. As my dad would say, "We want to eat filet mignon on a hamburger salary."

The need to compete and impress (comparative influences) contribute to the consuming habits that lead us into debt. King Solomon stated *(paraphrasing)* that the reason people work so hard is that they are driven by envy of their neighbors. Envy, greed, and the need to stay ahead is meaningless and can be compared to chasing the wind. [25] In other words, people are in constant pursuit of things that can't be "caught." They are chasing things that in the end will never satisfy them. And much like the wind, if the chase for "things" becomes strong, it can wreak havoc in your life.

For the undisciplined consumer, using credit is borrowing from your future self. The danger in borrowing from your future is that you have no idea what the future holds. We assume that our resources will be status quo or better. I've known individuals who were up to their eyeballs in credit card and other debt and seemed to be "successfully" managing their finances. However, as life would have it, a job loss caused them to lose most of their income. Without a fully-funded emergency savings account, the debt situation grew worse.

Unnecessary debt shows a lack of faith in God's ability to provide. Instead of waiting for God's blessings in your life or trusting him to give you the desires of your heart, you jump the gun and acquire those "blessings" on your own. Then you claim that God has been good to allow you to get those things that you struggle to pay for. Those are not blessings. God will not bless you with things that cause you to struggle and become miserable trying to manage. God's blessings do not bring sorrow.[26]

You may be wondering if it's ever okay to use credit or debt. No one knows you better than you know yourself. If you know that you don't have the self-control or discipline to monitor your spending so that you only purchase what you can afford to pay in full at the end of the month, then you should not use credit cards.

Credit or debt should only be used for things that appreciate, such as a mortgage for a home loan or student loans. Student loans can be considered an investment if you make wise decisions concerning your choice of schools and the amount of loans to take out. The idea of using credit for appreciating items is that the value of the item purchased with the loan will increase more than the total interest paid for the item. This is typically the case with real estate because in most cases you gain on your investment.

It's never a good idea to use credit for things that depreciate or are consumed, like clothing, cars, and food. If there is no anticipation of a return on your purchase, you should not use credit to acquire the item. You might ask, "What about your electronic gadgets, happy hour tabs, restaurant bills, furniture, and vacations?" Are you supposed to pay cash for these things? That's so un-American, right? You put these things on credit cards because you want them immediately. You certainly can't go to the concert in the same outfit you wore to the comedy show last month. You can't continue using your same cell phone once the two-year contract is up—a new cell phone every two years is a must have. And who carries cash anymore? Just charge the happy hour drinks and dinner bill to the credit card.

Aunt Betty and Uncle Joe are visiting next week, and you know how uppity they can be—you *have* to replace that raggedy couch. Your child is turning five years old next month and the celebration has got to be off the chain—after all, the pictures for social media must be on point. What will people think otherwise? You've just finished paying off your six-year-old Toyota Camry that still runs perfectly. Suddenly, it no longer fits your needs. So, you use the money you just freed up from paying off your car debt to finance your dream luxury car because the style suits you better.

These and similar scenarios have played out all too often. The sum of all these behaviors is what has caused many of you to become financially depleted. In Proverbs 22:7, King Solomon warns that those who are in debt are slaves to the lenders. Slaves are not free to make their own choices. They are bound by their master who sets limitations on what they can do. When you are heavily burdened with debt, it serves as your master and you are under its control. The things you want to do and places you want to go are off limits. Why? Because your master (debt) says that you can't afford it. The master says that you must pay him first—he's now your priority. You want to save for retirement, college, or to start your business, but the master says, "No, pay me first." King Solomon says to "free" yourself from this trap by working diligently and then run as fast as a gazelle to get away from it.[27] In other words, do not live with debt hanging over your head. Get rid of it as quickly as possible. Get on a debt elimination plan and be consistent in working the plan.

Using credit irresponsibly and struggling to pay off enormous amounts of debt can affect every area of your life. Relationships suffer because of debt. Money conflicts are one of the primary causes of relationship or marital discord. When couples don't see eye-to-eye on finances, it can wreak havoc in the relationship. One spouse may be frugal and the other may be a spender. If the spender is constantly running up the charge cards and getting the family further in debt, this is a sign of selfishness and lack of respect for the family goals. Excessive spending and non-commitment to the household financial goals cause repeated arguments. The arguments lead to financial infidelity—hiding and lying about spending and other financial matters. These behaviors lead to a breakdown of communications, disrespect, and loss of intimacy. Unfortunately, many marriages do not survive this level of conflict and mistrust.

Some individuals are so deep in debt that it causes their health to suffer. The stress and anxiety over not knowing what bills can be paid and the seemingly insurmountable amount of debt can affect your physical health. Worries over debt and the feeling as if you can't see a way out may cause you to become depressed. The immune system is lowered with the onset of stress. Stress sets up the environment in your body to allow any propensity for illness to surface. It becomes a vicious cycle of observing what others have, acquiring those things using debt, and becoming more stressed and depressed. You feel hopelessly trapped.

Financial problems may affect your job. If you are stressed and depressed, it may cause you to be less effective at work. You begin missing deadlines, become withdrawn, take more sick days, and become generally disengaged. Others may notice your behavior changes and you may miss out on promotional opportunities.

Your spiritual life may also be affected by your credit/debt trap. As I briefly mentioned earlier, acquiring debt to meet your every need doesn't allow God to show you what real faith looks like. How will you learn to trust God for your provisions if your security is in your credit card? You must learn to trust not only God's perfect provisions but also His perfect timing.

The Bible tells us that every good and perfect gift comes from above,[28] and you learned earlier that God's blessings do not bring sorrow. You can trust yourself and the resources that have been entrusted to you and think that you have arrived by what you have been able to consume or collect. What you've accumulated by your own accord does not even come close to the satisfaction of what God will indeed bless you with if you give Him the opportunity. It will serve you well to learn to wait on Him because the blessings He gives are perfectly designed and orchestrated just for you.

Practicing delayed gratification and avoiding debt becomes easier as you begin to understand the value of who you are and what you were born to do. You were not born to see how quickly you can amass material stuff. In the grand scheme of things, God is not the least bit concerned with your stockpile of things. He's more concerned with what's in your heart and how you use those things. Living your best life requires you to make wise spending decisions. Live and spend as if you have a future.

One of the main reasons people get caught in the credit/debt trap is because they were never properly educated on the ins and outs of how credit works, its relationship to debt, or the ramifications of abuse. Credit itself is not a dangerous thing. However, much like a firearm or vehicle, if you don't learn how to handle it and follow proper procedures, it can be extremely dangerous, especially in the hands of someone who is irresponsible. The information that follows is intended to educate you on credit and debt so that if you choose to use it, you'll know how to do so responsibly.

Credit Scores

Credit scoring companies determine how much of a risk you are for borrowing money. FICO (Fair Issac & Company) is the more popular data analytics company focused on credit scoring. FICO scores range from 300 to 850. Lenders interpret these scores to mean the following:

FICO Score	Typical Meaning
800 and up	Exceptional: You'll have a good chance of getting loans at the best interest rates. These loans may require less documentation and less or no down payment, collateral or co-signer. 1% delinquency rate.
740-799	Very Good: You'll usually be able to negotiate good terms. 2% delinquency rate.
670-739	Good: You'll be in a "standard" class of borrowers which means you'll have less flexibility in choosing better loans or services. 8% delinquency rate.
580-669	Fair (subprime): You'll be viewed by creditors with a critical eye and may need a co-signer to be approved for most loans and services. 28 % delinquency rate.
Under 580	Poor (subprime): You'll typically be required to provide a substantial down payment/collateral and pay the highest interest rate. 61% delinquency rate.

You should obtain a copy of your credit report each year. You're entitled to a free credit report from all three reporting agencies at www.annualcreditreport.com. Your credit score is important because it determines how much money you will pay to borrow money (interest). Interest is calculated as an APR or annual percentage rate. If your APR on a loan is 18%, the monthly interest you pay on the outstanding balance of your loan is 1.5% (18 APR/12 months = 1.5%). The higher your balances, the more you're paying for the loan.

Below is an illustration showing why it's important to maintain a healthy credit score:

Jim's Credit Score is 800		Pam's Credit Score is 590	
Car Loan	$15,000	Car Loan	$15,000
Term	60 months	Term	60 months
Interest Rate	6%	Interest Rate	18%
Total Interest	$2,288	Total Interest	$6,862
Total Cost	$17,288	Total Cost	$21,862

These two borrowers purchased cars that cost the same and they made monthly payments for five years. However, because Pam's credit score was considerably lower than Jim's, the lender offered her an interest rate significantly higher. Pam ends up paying $4,574 more for her car. If you must use credit, you'll want to get the lowest interest rate possible—and that depends on your credit score.

What Makes Up Your Credit Score?

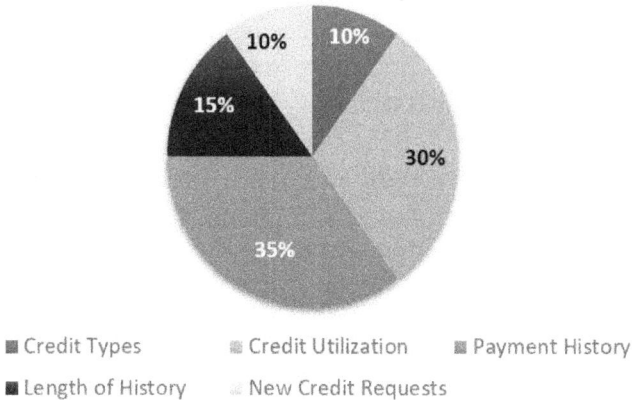

■ Credit Types   ▦ Credit Utilization   ▨ Payment History
■ Length of History   ▨ New Credit Requests

Your credit score is derived from information in your credit report. The information is weighted into five categories:

- **35%   Payment History:** the ability to make consistent, timely payments over a length of time. This is the most critical area to work on when fixing your score. Pay your bills on time every time.

- **30%   Credit Utilization:** the measure of total credit used to total credit available. For example, if the total credit limit for all your accounts total $20,000 and your outstanding debt balances total $10,000, you are utilizing 50% of your available credit. Your score will start to be affected when your utilization rate exceeds 30%. Paying off debt will decrease your utilization rate and may boost your score.

- **15%   Age of Credit History:** the longer you have a credit account, the better. When paying off balances, do not close the accounts. Cut the cards up and commit to not using the account. Closing the accounts erases your history and increases your utilization rate by reducing the available credit.

- **10%   New Credit History:** multiple requests for a credit account over a brief period, typically within a 6-month period. This is an indicator that you are perhaps getting in way over your head. Inquiries that you initiate to apply for credit remain on your report for two years.

- **10%   Types of Credit:** A mix of varying types of credit, such as revolving credit (accounts where the available amount of credit is increased and decreased as credit is used and repaid—credit cards), and installment credit (accounts that are closed once the loan is paid in full—car loan). Reporting agencies like to know that you can responsibly handle multiple types of credit arrangements. Do not try to develop a perfect mix in the hopes of raising your score. This opens the door for foolishness. This category is only 10% of your score so it's not that serious.

Count the Cost of Credit

If you choose to use credit, you should count the cost. There are certain "rules," that must be followed to prevent an unhealthy credit score. The rules include paying bills on time and not carrying balances. When credit bills are not paid timely, and if you are paying the minimum amount due and carrying balances on your credit cards, you may as well be throwing money in the trash.

The chart below illustrates the effects of interest and how long it will take you to pay off a balance of $1,500 paying the minimum of $30, compared to adding an additional $30 and $40. Assume an APR of 11% and no additional charges.

Monthly Payment	Months to Pay Off	Total Interest Paid	Total Paid
$30 (min)	68	$515.73	$2,015.73
$60	29	$211.54	$1,711.54
$100	17	$121.13	$1,621.13

If you can find extra money to apply toward your monthly payment, you'll pay your credit card balance off much sooner. In this example, applying just $70 more per month to the minimum will pay the card off in a year and a half as opposed to five years and save $394.60 in interest!

Repairing Bad Credit

Credit repair services offer a valuable service of convenience. However, they can cost upwards of $300. Many individuals use these services because they don't have the time or possess the skills to adequately communicate their message to the credit reporting agencies. If you have patience and are willing to do the work yourself, you can save money by following the steps below:

1. Request a copy of your credit report from each of the three credit reporting agencies. You can receive all three reports (Equifax, TransUnion, and Experian) at annualcreditreport.com, or by calling 1-811-322-8228. Your report will give you a clear picture of your current credit status so you can determine what needs to be done.

2. Review the reports for inaccuracies. Review your personal identifying information—name spelling, social security number, etc. Review each account thoroughly and highlight all errors so that you don't forget to include them in your dispute letters.

3. Write a letter of dispute to each of the agencies. If the same error appears on more than one report, you must address the error with each of the agencies separately. You can dispute inaccuracies in writing via a letter (I would send a certified letter), or you may also file a dispute online. In either case, be sure to include any documentation that supports your dispute. Instructions for filing disputes are included in your credit report.

Your communication should identify the error and include an explanation of why you feel the entry is inaccurate. List the items you're including as supporting documentation. A sample letter can be found at www.consumer.ftc.gov/articles/0384-sample-letter-disputing-errors-your-credit-report.

Four things you can do to boost your credit score:

1. Pay your bills on time, every time.
2. Pay down your debt balances to decrease your utilization ratio.
3. Identify and dispute all errors on your credit report.
4. Avoid applying for multiple credit accounts within a 12-month period.

Student Loan Debt

Student loan debt is the largest debt carried after home mortgages. Many people are struggling to meet the requirements of the loan repayment terms and some people simply give up paying altogether. Student loan payment obligations are a major cause of young adults delaying the transition to true adulthood and independence. Consider the following:

- Average student loan debt is $39,400[29]
- Delinquency rate is 12%
- Average monthly payment is $351
- Average time to pay off the loan balance is ten years

If you're finding it difficult to manage your student loan payments, below are options to consider:

1. Opt for a lower interest rate. Check with your loan servicer to see if they offer automatic payments. Your interest rate may be decreased by 0.25% which will lower your payments and total interest paid.

2. Pause your payment. *Deferment:* Suspends your payments and interest (on some loans) for events such as continued education, unemployment, and economic hardship. *Forbearance:* Suspends your payments, but NOT your interest. Note: There is an option to capitalize your interest (have it added to the loan balance). However, this may cause you to pay more interest over time.

3. Change your due date or your repayment plan. *Change due date:* Scheduling your payment due date to coincide with your employer's pay date will ensure the money is available and your account is paid on time which may increase your credit score.

NOTE: Many student loan debt scammers attempt to convince student loan holders that they can help manage or get rid of their student loans. Scammers will ask for a fee for their services. You should not pay any fees to restructure or consolidate your loans. You can receive free debt relief services for federal loans at studentloans.gov.

Options for Funding College without Student Loans

- Consider school choice. Community colleges and trade schools are less expensive.
- Work and save for college before attending.
- Work while attending college, even if you must attend part-time. Pay cash as you go.
- Live at home or with a roommate to save money.
- Take online courses which are usually significantly cheaper.
- Apply for scholarships and grants.
- Consider military service which provides opportunities to attend college virtually for free.

Many college students don't consider future financial implications when choosing a college major. They borrow more than their future income will allow them to repay without difficulty. For example, if your major is elementary education, you would not assume $80,000 of student loan debt. If you choose to borrow (and I certainly hope you don't), borrow only the amount of your anticipated beginning annual salary. Following this rule of thumb ensures that the repayments are manageable and that you'll pay it off in a reasonable amount of time. In our teacher example, $80,000 would be too much student loan debt considering the national average salary for elementary school teachers is $44,000.[30]

Parents—do not allow your 18-year old to make choices that are clearly going to yield negative financial consequences. Educate them on the importance of choosing the right school based on the funds available through savings or scholarships. Discourage them from choosing a school because of its popularity or because their friends are attending. The important thing is that the school has the area of study for their intended major. In fact, save money by sending them to a community college for the first two years to complete their general courses. If you ask most individuals who are struggling with student loan payments what regrets they have, the resounding answers would be that they regret taking out more student loans than they needed, and they would have chosen a less expensive school.

Mortgage Debt

Before purchasing a home, consider if it is something you really want to do and that you're not just doing it because you think that's what you're *supposed* to do at this stage in your life. Home ownership is a good thing and can be a great investment if you do it the right way. This includes being mature enough to handle the responsibility of owning property and being financially prepared.

I can't tell you how many stories I've listened to where someone's so-called *blessing* of a home became their financial nightmare. They have a big beautiful home but can't afford to furnish it or pay the bills that come with a house of that size. They also can't enjoy other things in life because all their money is tied up in mortgage payments. In many cases, the buyers had too little savings to cover emergencies. These situations can cause the homeowner to go further into debt just to take care of the basics. In a nutshell, these homeowners are house poor.

You may want to think twice about purchasing a home if you have a job that requires you to relocate every few years, such as a military member. I've witnessed individuals who purchased homes and were soon faced with the decision to sell or rent the home when it came time for them to relocate. Many times, the homes were purchased in new development areas. This made it difficult to sell the home because buyers were able to purchase a new home for the same list price of the home being sold.

You can rent the property out, but history has shown that most long-distance landlord situations do not turn out well and can be expensive when you consider that you must pay someone to manage the property. You must also pay for any necessary repairs—no matter how many times the tenant's kid breaks the windows or how often the drains get clogged. And then there's the carpet replacement and painting between each rental agreement. The lesson here is that if you are transient and decide to purchase a home, you should be financially prepared for the expenses that come with selling or renting your home

Buying a home is a huge responsibility. It is not as simple as trading rent for mortgage payments. Before purchasing a home, consider the following:

1. **Build your emergency fund**. Make sure you have a fully-funded emergency savings account consisting of three to six months of expenses. This will ensure that you are able to make your mortgage payments if you're faced with a loss of income. The fund also covers you for a period if you should have to suddenly move and pay housing for two places until you get a buyer or tenant.

2. **Save for a down payment.** The typical down payment is 20% of the purchase price. This will prevent you from having to pay PMI-Private Mortgage Insurance which protects the lender from loss in the event you default on the loan (foreclosure). PMI is typically .5% to 1% of the loan amount. A $100,000 loan at 1% would add an additional $83 to your monthly mortgage payment ($1,000/12 months). PMI is different from homeowner's insurance which protects the homeowner. You will pay

PMI until you've built up about 20% equity. Equity is the amount of money that would come to you after paying the lender the balance due on the loan when the house is sold. If you assume a 30-year mortgage, you must make payments for five years before PMI can be cancelled.

3. Choose a 15-year mortgage only. The difference you'll pay in interest compared to a 30-year mortgage is significant. A $200,000 home for 15 years at 4% will cost you only $66,288 in interest. The same loan for 30 years will cost you $143,739 in interest. You'll pay a slightly higher monthly mortgage for the 15-year mortgage, but you'll be finished paying for your home much sooner. Having no mortgage payment means you'll have more money for other financial goals. If you're an older purchaser and opt for a 30-year mortgage, you may be carrying that large monthly bill well into your retirement years when your income is likely to be lower and fixed.

4. Limit monthly mortgage payments to 25-30% of your net income. Principal and insurance should be included in the monthly payment as part of the 25% to 30 % of your net income (take-home pay). If you exceed 30%, you may not be able to meet other financial obligations without making major lifestyle adjustments or going further into debt to maintain your current lifestyle.

You should have your budget established so you can determine the monthly mortgage payment you can afford. Your home purchase should be based on what your budget will allow. Don't shop for your dream home and then try to force the monthly payment into your budget. Some realtors may try to get you into a home that you love but can't easily afford. It makes no sense to be in your dream home and not be able to buy furniture or pay the utilities.

I was 31 years old when I purchased my first home. My husband and I were being reassigned to Peterson Air Force Base in Colorado Springs, CO. Having been pre-approved for our loan before arriving, we started house hunting immediately. We gave the realtor our house budget. He began showing us homes that were selling for much more than we wanted to pay. After about three or four showings, I'd finally had enough and asked him why he was showing us homes out of our budget. He looked surprised and said that our pre-qualification documents indicated that we were qualified for $100,000 more than the price we gave him. He assumed we would purchase a home for the maximum amount the lender was willing to loan. We had a budget, and *we* were telling our money where we wanted it to go.

The lender and the realtor may have their own interest in your home purchase. The more you spend on a home, the bigger the commission the realtor gets and the more interest the lender makes. Don't allow them to tell you where your money should go. You are in charge. Long story short, we found a home that we loved and was priced within our budget. The home was also much bigger than we anticipated. When we transferred four years later, we sold the home immediately and pocketed $25,000—not a bad return on our investment. Our frugality allowed us to enjoy our time in Colorado because our money was not tied up in huge mortgage payments. Again, I caution you about purchasing your primary home if you have a transient job. The housing market happened to be doing well at the time we sold our home in Colorado. As with any other investment, you should always research the market and consider your personal circumstances before making a commitment.

Debt Payoff Plan

The snowball payoff method. I first learned of this plan through Dave Ramsey's radio show. The way it works is that you'll list all your debt balances from smallest to largest, ignoring the applicable interest rates. This includes all debt (credit cards, car loan, student loans, and personal loans) except your mortgage. Once you have all your debt balances listed, you'll pay the minimum amount due on all the balances except the smallest. For the smallest balance, you will pay as much as your budget will allow above the minimum payment. You may have to make some sacrifices, such as giving up eating out so often or cutting back on other non-essential expenses. Add the money saved to the minimum payment of your smallest balance. Once you get that balance paid off, you'll add the money you were paying on the previous smallest balance to the minimum payment of the next smallest balance. Repeat the process until all your debt is paid.

EXAMPLE: The Smiths have $27,000 in debt and have decided to add $100 more per month to their debt payment plan. Their debt is broken out as follows (interest is listed for comparison of total costs):

Credit Card 1	$1,000	11.5%	Min $25
Credit Card 2	$1,500	10%	Min $30
Credit Card 3	$3,000	11%	Min $60
Personal Loan	$3,500	14%	Min $70
Car Loan	$6,000	8%	Min $250
Student Loan	$12,000	3.5%	Min 350

They will begin paying $125 on credit card one ($25 minimum plus $100 extra). After ten months, they will be done with Credit Card 1. They now have $125 to add to the $30 minimum payment on Credit Card 2 which increases the monthly payment to $155.

After 19 months, they are done with Credit Card 2 and can now add $155 to the $60 minimum payment for Credit Card 3 for a total of $215. At the end of this pattern, the Smith's will have paid off their entire debt in only 2.83 years and paid $3,071 in interest. Had they not snowballed their debt and continued to pay the minimum payment due on each account, it will have taken them nearly 6.5 years and cost them $4,753 in interest. What a difference a $100 sacrifice makes! Of course, the debt snowball payoff plan assumes you won't be accumulating more debt along the way—no more charges on the credit cards and no more taking out loans. You must be done with credit for your plan to be successful. To see how long it will take you to pay off your debt using the snowball method, use the snowball debt calculator at https://www.nerdwallet.com/blog/finance/debt-snowball-calculator/.

When people say they will never be able to pay off their student loans and have accepted them as a lifelong sentence, I tell them all they need to do is get a plan and be consistent. It can be done. For amazing testimonies of how others have paid off their student loans in record time, a simple YouTube search of "how I paid off my student loans" will yield tons of encouraging videos. You will notice the common themes of these success stories are commitment, sacrifice, and consistency.

To live your best life, you must make a firm decision that you are no longer going to be a slave to debt. Debt will not control your life, make decisions for you, or restrict you. Debt will not continue to rob your financial future. You have better things to do than spend your precious time living beneath your financial potential. You have places to go, dreams to fulfill, and a legacy to build.

Other Methods of Managing Debt

Other popular choices for eliminating debt are listed below. However, I do not recommend any of them as the best choice for a debt elimination plan. These methods are designed to be quick fixes that may end up costing you more. Often, when things are "fixed" quickly, we don't learn the lessons that prevent us from being in a bad place. When you work a plan consistently over time, you develop a different mindset, form different habits, and you're less likely to repeat bad behaviors. Unless you come to terms with the behaviors that landed you in a debt situation in the first place, it's only a matter of time before you find yourself right back in the same situation. When it comes to using the equity in your home to pay off debt, there is the possibility that you may lose your home. Debt Settlement and Bankruptcy are viewed as equally "bad" when it comes to assessing your credit risk. These "solutions" are reported to the credit bureaus and adversely affect your credit score.

Debt Consolidation: The process of combining multiple loan accounts into one account to better manage the payments. The consolidated loan typically has a lower rate, but in most cases, the terms are extended causing you to pay more on the loan overall than you would have with the individual loan accounts.

Debt Settlement: The process of hiring a company who specializes in negotiating with creditors to get your payments reduced. Debt settlement companies are known for scams and the service can be expensive. Any debt you settle will be reported to the credit bureaus and have an adverse effect on your credit score. You will pay taxes on the amount of debt forgiven.

Balance Transfers: Transferring high-interest rate credit card balances to another credit card with a limited duration zero interest rate. Transferees will pay a fee equal to 3% of the total amount of balances transferred. The zero interest applies to the transferred balances only. Any additional purchases made on the card will have the standard credit card interest rate applied. If the balance transferred is not paid off during the offer period, you will begin paying interest accrued from the first day of the transfer.

Employer Tax Advantage Retirement Plan Loan: Borrowing from your 401(k), 403(b), or 457 retirement plan. These plans typically allow you to borrow from your account and give you up to five years to repay with interest. However, if your job should end for any reason, you must pay the total amount due within 60 days of termination. In addition, missed payments may result in taxes and penalties. You'll also miss out on growth opportunities. The interest you're paying to yourself is typically not more than the returns you would have made.

Home Equity Loan: Borrowing against the equity in your home using your home as collateral. Borrowers can get up to 80% of the home's equity. People assume these one-time lump sum loans to pay off other debt because the interest is usually lower. Interest rates are fixed so the monthly payment stays the same until the loan is paid off. Fees can be expensive. The biggest risk is that the borrower can lose their home if they are not able to repay the loan.

Home Equity Line of Credit (HELOC): An open line of credit for a maximum amount for a certain period. It functions like a credit card. You pay interest on the amount borrowed at any given time. There are many restrictions and fees involved with HELOCs. Also, the rates are variable so the amount of your monthly payment may fluctuate. Your home is collateral, and you can lose it if you're not able to repay the loan.

Bankruptcy: A court adjudication process where you are either relieved of all eligible debt or you can restructure your debt and make lower payments. Biblical principles dictate that people who do not pay their debts are wicked.[31] That sounds pretty harsh, huh? The point is that bankruptcy should be the last resort when it comes to settling debt and should be used only for extreme circumstances. An example would be a situation where a person may be physically or mentally disabled with limited resources and is in jeopardy of losing their home.

To get ahead, you must avoid going into debt for things that will not provide any future benefits. If you must enter debt, assume only as much as it takes to accomplish the task and then pay it off as quickly as possible. Don't over borrow for education or housing. Finally, have a plan for paying off debt *before* you assume it.

The rate at which you get rid of your debt is directly related to the level of sacrifices you're willing to make. You can choose to change your spending habits, rethink your priorities, and fund your future. Or, you can continue enjoying temporary pleasures and chasing the wind with no regard for your future or your legacy. Living with debt doesn't have to be the norm. You can't live your best life when your resources are continuously diverted to debt. Free your money up so you can get on with the business of being the person you were called to be and doing that which you were called to do.

Step 4 - Avoid the Credit and Debt Trap

Step 5 - Save and Invest

The wise store up choice food and olive oil, but fools gulp theirs (Proverbs 21:20)

Most Americans are not prepared to handle an emergency that would require money to resolve. According to a 2017 GoBankingRates survey, 57% of Americans have less than $1,000 in savings. And a whopping 36% of those individuals have nothing saved at all.[32] Most people are living paycheck to paycheck which means a typical emergency would leave them financially depleted.

At the very least, you should find a way to create and maintain an emergency fund because guess what? The car *is* going to break down. The water heater *will* begin leaking. Someone *will* die requiring you to travel long distance. You or your kid *will* have an accident requiring medical attention. The bottom line is that stuff happens.

In December 2018, more than 800,000 people working for the federal government had the rug pulled from under them when the government shut down for 33 days. Many of these individuals had no income during that time and were relegated to getting assistance from community food banks. I'm almost certain that many of those affected had little to no emergency savings.

Disasters such as hurricanes, snow storms, and wildfires are events that many people are not prepared to handle. Whether your emergency is as small as needing a set of tires for your car or reeling from a major natural disaster, they both disrupt your life. Having no financial resources will prevent you from recovering timely. Your emergency savings is a self-funded insurance policy to help you manage the inevitable without going into debt.

Living your best life requires you to anticipate and prepare for the unexpected. It's not a matter of *if* you'll have an emergency, but when. If you're not prepared, you'll be forced to borrow money from a friend, relative, use a credit card, or take out a loan—all of which create debt.

Most everyday emergencies, such as a car repair or emergency room visit should not cost more than $1,000 to resolve. This is the recommended amount for you to put away in a money market fund at your credit union or bank. If $1,000 seems too big of a burden, start with $100 or whatever you can afford. Consistently add to the fund until you reach your target. This $1,000 is your designated "baby" emergency fund. Once you eliminate your debt, except for your mortgage, you'll want to save at least three to six months of expenses as your fully-grown emergency fund. For now, your focus should be on paying off debt and keeping your baby emergency fund intact. Once your emergency is resolved, replenish the fund to the full amount.

If you're not sure what constitutes an emergency, let me be clear. An emergency is an unexpected event that threatens life, safety, or security and must be resolved immediately. Most emergencies will be the sudden car or home repair that can't wait, such as plumbing or electrical issues, failed major appliances (refrigerator), or a medical mishap.

Your favorite music group coming to your city is not an emergency, and neither is the new outfit you were planning to buy for the concert. The item you've been eyeing for six months that finally goes on sale is not an emergency. Your friends announcing a weekend get-a-way is not an emergency. Two-for-one drinks at happy hour is definitely not an emergency. I'm sure you get the point. Know the difference.

One important thing to keep in mind is that your emergency fund is *your* emergency fund. Everyone else's emergency cannot be yours. If the same people are repeatedly tapping into your fund, that's a sign that they may not be managing their money properly. You are not responsible for being the safety net for stupidity. Use wisdom and learn to discern when people genuinely need your help.

If someone asks you for money, you have every right to ask how the money will be used so that you can determine, by your standards, if the situation is a real emergency. Remember, you must replenish the fund so that it's available when *you* need it.

Why don't most people have an emergency fund? In many cases, it's due to bad spending choices. These choices may be symptoms of larger issues such as the need to please and impress and the barriers I spoke about in Step Three—lack of self- control and the unwillingness to practice delayed gratification. The mentality of YOLO—you only live once— has become so prevalent and people fail to realize that they really do live only once. If you're like most people, you desire to live well beyond your retirement years. If you're spending more money than you make, what's left to save for those years when you aren't working? Saving should be a top priority if you want to live your best life, not just for today, but living the best life possible during your retirement. To do that, you must learn to live beneath your means. You cannot have more money going out than what's coming in. It's pure mathematics—you will not get ahead.

One way to find money to establish your emergency fund or to save for other goals is to curtail your spending. Most people can find something they routinely purchase or an activity they can sacrifice for this greater cause. In addition to decreasing spending, you can increase your income by taking on a side hustle. Think about things you can do to generate extra income. Do you have a skill you can monetize, such as consulting, photography, braiding hair, tutoring, or singing?

As part of a personal finance class that I teach at my place of employment, I ask students to write one goal they would like to achieve but have not done so because of financial challenges. I tell them to focus on that goal as we go through the course and think about how the topics we cover can help them achieve their goal. My objective is to help them realize that their goal or dream is attainable if they are willing to make adjustments in their spending and saving practices. At the end of the course, many of them are encouraged and excited to begin putting the concepts into practice. It warms my heart when someone who attended my class approaches me with an unsolicited progress report enthusiastically stating that they've established their emergency fund or paid off two, three, or all their credit cards!

Below are examples of temporary sacrifices that may help to build your savings:

Spending Habits	Approx. Monthly Savings
daily gourmet coffee	$80
daily breakfast sandwich purchase	$70
eating out for lunch	$200
daily soft drink	$32
manicure/pedicure	$60
weekly happy hour	$100

Changing just these habits alone has the potential to save you over $500. Think about the things you could do with an extra $500 each month. Miriam Caldwell provides 100 additional ways to save money at www.thebalance.com/ways-to-save-money-this-year-2386116. I challenge you to find five things from Miriam's list that you can start practicing today.

Where to Save Your Money

Once you decide that saving money is a critical part of your financial planning, there are several options to consider. Short-term savings for things like your emergency fund should be deposited at a Federal Deposit Insurance Cooperation (FDIC) backed financial institution like a bank or credit union. The FDIC insures your deposits up to $250,000 in the event the bank goes belly up. Do not keep your emergency money in a shoebox, coffee can or under the mattress where it is not safe and has no potential for growth. You also don't want your money to be easily accessible so that you're tempted to use it for non-emergency events. The following account types are available at most financial institutions:

Basic Savings Account (average interest as of 11/18/18 was .08%)

Checking Account (it is rare for a bank to pay interest on a checking account, but for those that do, the average rate is .05%)

Money Market Account (interest rate of .08% to .11%, depending on the size of the deposit)

Certificate of Deposit (CD) interest rates vary depending on the amount of the CD but averages between 1% and 3%. The larger your CD amount and the longer it's held, the larger the interest rate.

The basic savings account is meant to hold your deposits for a substantial length of time. It is not intended to be transactional like your checking account from which you make frequent deposits and withdrawals for everyday financial needs. Your debit card is tied to your checking account when used at a point of sale (cash register when making purchases). However, if you use the card at an ATM teller, you have the option of withdrawing from your checking or savings account.

Money Market accounts serve as a longer-term savings account and pay a tiny bit more interest than a regular savings account. Banks make money by issuing loans. The money for these loans comes from customer deposits. The longer they hold your deposits, the more money they have available to loan to other customers. As an incentive for keeping your money on deposit, banks pay you a slightly higher interest rate than you would earn on a regular savings account. They also place restrictions on the number of withdrawals you can make within a certain period. Fees usually apply if you exceed the limit.

A Certificate of Deposit is an even longer-term savings account. It's a promissory note issued by the bank that agrees to pay you a higher interest rate if you agree to keep the deposit for a set amount of time. The longer the term, the more interest you're paid. Most banks require a minimum deposit amount of $1,000 to be held for 6 to 60 months. The biggest downfall to a CD is the forfeiture of the interest earned if you withdraw the funds before it matures (reaches its term).

I use CDs for my emergency fund and stagger the terms of maturity. For example, I have deposits on 1, 5, and 10-year terms. The bank sends a notice before the CD matures, and I can decide at that time whether to release the funds from the CD or allow it to continue with the same terms. Some banks give you the option to have your CD automatically roll over to a higher rate if a better rate is available when your CD matures. Financial institutions differ in their rules and restrictions so check with your institution for more information.

Investing

Remember the Bible story from Step One about the servant who buried the money instead of investing it? His excuse was that he was afraid. Apparently, he deemed that the master would be angry if he risked losing the money. While the other servants invested the money given to them and yielded a return for the master, this servant did nothing out of fear. Because he did nothing, he lost the money given to him. Maximizing the resources God gives us is not only beneficial, but it's also expected.

For those major life events that happen "down the road" such as college and retirement, you must figure out the best way to fund these events. You can't wait until the day of reckoning and expect the resources you need to be available. With the average student loan debt being $39,400, ask any young person who is shouldering this burden if they wish their parents had saved more for their college education. Ask one of the many retirees forced to forego a leisurely life of retirement if they wish they had started investing earlier in their working years. The answer to both questions would be a resounding yes.

We see retirees working every day as we shop at Walmart, eat at McDonald's, or attend a live stage show. They are our greeters, table wipers, and ushers. Not all retirees who work are in dire need of money—some work to continue to be socialized. But far more of them work because they have to—not because they *want* to. They are definitely not living their best lives because they did not prepare financially. If you have not yet started planning for college or retirement, what are you waiting for?

To start saving and investing, you could place your money in a regular saving, money market, or CD account. While banking accounts are minimal risk, you won't receive the returns you'll need to fund your retirement or your child's education.

Consider Rule 72. This rule is a simplified way to determine how long it takes for an investment to double. To figure how long it will take $1,000 to double at 1% interest (which is what banks are typically paying these days), you would divide the number 72 by the interest rate of 1%. If you place your money in a regular savings account at 1% interest, it will take 72 years for that $1,000 to become $2,000. Who has 72 years to play around with this stuff? I recommend using bank accounts to secure your emergency funds only. You don't want to take any risks with money that's designated for emergencies. You also want those funds to be readily available when you need them.

For long-term savings that yield much better returns, you may want to consider investing your money in mutual funds. Company sponsored plans, such as the 401(k), and individual retirement accounts—Traditional and ROTH—invest in mutual funds. A mutual fund pools money from different investors to purchase a large group of assets (stocks and bonds). The fund is professionally managed, meaning someone makes decisions on buying and selling the assets. The fund manager makes money through fees which are a small percentage of the account balance. Therefore, it's in the fund manager's best interest to manage the fund as smartly as possible. The bigger the fund balance, the more money they make.

The most significant benefit of mutual fund investing is that your investments are diversified. In other words, you're not placing all your eggs in one basket. King Solomon speaks of the importance of diversification in the Bible. He advises that we should invest in multiple areas because we don't know which ones will prosper.[33]

Mutual funds are invested in multiple companies and assets (stocks and bonds). If one company does poorly, the others in the fund may be doing well. This differs from single stock investing where you could lose everything if the company goes bad. Diversifying your investments decreases the chance for big losses. Investors in a mutual fund share equally in losses and wins.

Let's revisit rule 72 again. The average mutual fund yields anywhere between 4% and 11 %. If we go in the middle, say 8%, it would take only nine years for that $1,000 to double. That's a significant difference from the 72 years it would take for the money to double if placed in a regular savings account.

The key to maximizing your investments is to start investing as early as possible so that you take advantage of the compounding effect. With compounding, your account earns interest on top of interest. Over time, your funds grow exponentially. Consider the following example:

Janae and Rasheed both contribute $200 each month to their employers 401(k) plan. They both plan to retire at the age of 67. However, Janae started contributing when she was 25 years old.

After attending a personal finance workshop, Rasheed, who is 40 years old, realized that he needed to get on the ball. At retirement, Janae will have contributed a total of $100,800. Because Rasheed started late, his total contributions will be $64,800. Assuming a rate of return of 8%, Janae's retirement fund will grow to $788,599, whereas Rasheed's retirement fund will grow to only $268,723. Time is the most critical aspect of building wealth through stock market investing. The earlier you start, the better off you'll be.

You should understand that the stock market fluctuates, and you must be patient and emotionally prepared to ride the ups and downs of the market. At the height of the 2008 recession, one of my employees, who was nearing retirement, shared with me that she was no longer contributing to her deferred compensation account. She'd been nervously studying her statements and watching her account balance decrease rapidly. She asked what I would do in her situation. I always hesitate to give advice of this nature because that's not my area of certification. I lovingly advised her to talk to our deferred compensation representative. She then asked what I was going to do. I told her that I was in it for the long haul. After all, I had at least 16 years before considering retirement. In fact, I increased my contributions so that I could get more shares at bargain prices. She ended up stopping her contributions out of fear that she would lose it all before she retired.

If you're nearing retirement or if college is around the corner, you might want to be more conservative with your investments. I recommend that you consult with a certified, fiduciary financial planner for personalized investment advice based on your situation.

So, where should you begin your investment journey? For starters, you're going to first work on clearing up your debt. Why? Because your debt is holding money hostage that you can use to contribute to your investment savings. You want as much money as possible to start *earning* interest as opposed to *paying* interest to your creditors.

After you get rid of the debt, if you have the option to participate in an employer contribution plan, you'll want to take advantage of it. Most employers will match your contributions up to a certain percentage of your salary. If the match is 3%, at the very least, you should contribute 3% of your salary to get the company match. If not, you're leaving free money on the table. If you contribute nothing, you get nothing. If you contribute at least 3%, you get 6% going into your investment account.

Employer-sponsored retirement plans are known as 401(k), 403(b), or 457 Plans and are named after the tax code under which they fall. Contributions are pre-tax and generally function the same way for private companies, non-profits, and governmental employers, respectively. Taxes are paid when the funds are distributed during retirement.

If your employer does not have a tax-deferred investment plan, the next best tools for investing are the Traditional Individual Retirement Account (IRA) or a ROTH IRA. Money in these retirement accounts are invested in mutual funds. The difference between the two is the timing of the taxes and the restrictions on withdrawals.

With a Traditional IRA, the contributions are made pretax which lowers your current tax liability. However, in most cases the withdrawals cannot happen before the age of 59 ½, and they are taxed at your tax rate at the time of withdrawal. If you withdraw before the age of eligibility, you will be assessed a 10% penalty in addition to the taxes. Contributions are fully, partially, or non-deductible depending on your income.

With a ROTH IRA, the contributions are made after taxes and are not deductible. However, the earnings continue to grow tax-free and there's no tax on your withdrawals in retirement. You can withdraw from your ROTH IRA anytime with no penalties, but if you withdraw the earnings (the money earned beyond your contributions), you may be taxed or penalized. You may also withdraw for qualified educational expenses.

Research these investment options as there may be other tax ramifications, fees, and restrictions. The bottom line is that you must be proactive in building the wealth you'll need to meet life's major milestones. If you don't do anything, you'll be like the servant that ended up with nothing because of his fear. If you want to have a pot of gold when you reach your golden years, you must start consistently dropping the nuggets in the pot.

Living your best life means that you make an effort to create peace and security for yourself and your children. The financial decisions you're making now will benefit your family today and for years to come. If you are planning for your children to go to college, you must also have a plan to pay for it. Your plan should not include taking on debt. Start a college savings fund as soon as possible.

Somehow, it has become acceptable to allow children to saddle themselves with student loan debt at the age of 18. These kids do not have any idea of the ramifications for signing on the dotted line basically signing their future away. Parents stand by cheering them on, not realizing that once these kids graduate—or not, they'll join the ranks of others who have an average of $39,400 in student loan debt hanging over their heads. Most college graduates do not get the job of their choice right out of college. Instead, they end up settling for what they can get because they must start paying back their student loans.

As mentioned earlier, the average monthly student loan payment is $351. Having to pay this amount each month severely delays the transition to adulthood for most college graduates. Many of them end up back home because they can't afford to pay rent. This debt also means they are marrying, starting families, and buying homes later in life. They can't save, invest, or prepare appropriately for emergencies. Student loan debt is a national crisis.

There is a better way to fund your child's education if you start early. Most states sponsor a tax advantage 529 plan. These plans were created to encourage parents to save for future educational needs. There are two types of programs—prepaid tuition plans and education savings plans.

A prepaid tuition plan allows the purchaser to buy college credits from a public in-state college or university at current prices which eliminates the worry of rising college costs because the prices are locked in. A plan can be purchased in a lump sum or through monthly payments over the number of years until the beneficiary enrolls in college. The younger the recipient when the plan is purchased, the smaller the monthly payments. The plans are funded through state governments and are not backed by the federal government.

Educational Savings Plans allow a saver to open an investment account for a designated beneficiary. The contributions are invested in various mutual fund portfolios. These funds are not subject to federal income tax and in many cases are not subject to a state tax if they're used for qualifying educational expenses.

Research both plans. There are restrictions, income limits, and rules on where the plans can be used. Check with your state's education department for more details.

The important thing is that you have a plan. We are responsible for providing for our children and that includes giving them the best education we can afford. Support and encourage your child to do their absolute best in school so they can compete for scholarships. Challenge them to participate in dual enrollment courses to earn college credit while in high school. Earning free college credits in high school means less college tuition costs. You should also steer them towards affordable schools and fields of study that will allow them to be self-supportive upon graduation. They cannot major in basket weaving and expect to be financially independent unless they choose a minimalistic lifestyle.

You are living your best life when you're confident that you have adequately prepared for your future, as well as that of your child. Knowing things are under control allows you to walk a little taller and breathe a little easier.

Step 5 - Save and Invest

Step 6 - Get a Plan

For which of you, desiring to build a tower, does not first sit down and count the cost, whether he has enough to complete it?   *(Luke 14:28)*

In 1975, Diana Ross starred in a movie titled *Mahogany,* in which she sang the theme song, *Do You Know Where You're Going To?*

Having always been a lover of words, I typically focus on the lyrics of a song. Even as a pre-teen, the lyrics of the song caused me to pause and wonder if I knew where my life was headed. In the song, Diana asks several questions.

> *Do you know where you're going to? Do you like the things that life is showing you?*
>
> *Where are you going to? Do you know?*
>
> *Do you get what you're hoping for when you look behind you there's no open doors?*
>
> *What are you hoping for? Do you know?*

Do you know where you're going, what you want, and more importantly, how you're going to make it happen? The truth is, many people can't answer any of Diana's questions. The reason is that they have not created a plan for their life. They get up every day, go to work, come home, watch television or play video games, go to bed, wake up and repeat. Meanwhile, their dreams are dying a slow death.

I talked about procrastination being one of the barriers to financial wellness, and I mentioned the brevity of life. Statistically speaking, we only get about 80 years of life.[34] So, if you're 40 years old, you have already spent 50 percent of your time here on earth. If you're 50-years old, you've spent 62%. The question is, what are you going to do with the remainder of your time? Time isn't going to stand still because you haven't yet "figured it out."

Too often, people overtalk, overthink, and overshare their plans or intentions. The problem is they never get around to doing anything to get the ball rolling. I once had a friend who seemed to be extremely ambitious. He regularly shared several business ideas he wanted to pursue. Every social event we attended, he would steer the conversation to the latest business adventure he was planning. He had grand plans—but they were stuck in his head. The sad thing is that he had the advantage over many aspiring entrepreneurs in that he was financially able to support each venture. Unfortunately, he never committed to a plan of action. Don't be the person who has great dreams and ideas only to let them die for lack of effort in creating a concrete plan.

Whatever you want to do in life, whether it's going back to school, start a business, get out of debt, or write a great novel, you must have a plan. If you don't create a plan, there's a great chance that:

1. You won't get the results you hoped to achieve.

2. It will take you longer to reach your goal.

3. Reaching your goal will cost you more financially.

Once you figure out what you want to do, write it down. God gave Moses the plan for man's successful living (The Ten Commandments) on a tablet—words he had written himself.[35] On another occasion, God instructed Habakkuk to write the vision of God's plan to intervene in a world gone evil. He told Habakkuk to make the vision plain so that there would be no misunderstanding of what was going to happen.[36] Using these examples, it's clear that writing clear goals serves as reminders and inspiration to follow through on the promises you make to yourself. Make your goals plain and simple so that you understand what needs to be done. If you focus on completing the first step of your plan, you'll be inspired to continue to the next step. Before you know it, you will have accomplished your goal. The greatest challenge in the process is getting started.

A major part of creating a plan for your life is incorporating a plan for your money. One of the biggest constraints to realizing dreams is the lack of money or what may be *perceived* as a lack of money. Often, it's the mismanagement of money. Many of you go about your daily business without a plan of how to spend, save, or give. Your idea of a budget is checking your account balance online every few days to gauge your financial status. You have no formal method of tracking or monitoring your spending. And you wonder why you can't get ahead or meet your financial goals. This is no way to manage money.

You need a written plan for your money, and that plan is called a budget. Creating a budget is the single most critical thing you can do to gain control of your finances. Get rid of any negative thoughts that tell you budgets are too restrictive or too hard, or that you don't have time to maintain a budget. A budget will put you in control of your money. If you don't control of your money, your money will control you.

The Bible emphasizes the importance of wise planning and the results of failing to do so. Jesus asks the question, "Who would start to build a tower or plan an attack without first sitting down to count the costs?" If you don't finish the task, you'll be ridiculed by others."[37] The ridicule will most likely be in the form of your regret. You may regret that you did not plan for a better outcome as you struggle to meet your life goals. You need a budget!

Most people have a finite amount of money coming into their household, and that money is usually enough to cover immediate needs—things needed for survival, safety, and security. Where they mess up is when they opt to fulfill their *wants* to the extent that their spending choices interfere with their ability to meet their future needs. What are you doing to secure your future financial needs? Are you saving or investing? Is your retirement fund growing? Are you making provisions for the needs of your loved ones for the day that you are no longer here? Most people do not think to include these needs in their financial planning. The financial plan that never makes it from the head to pen is no plan at all. Below are the steps to get you started with your plan of action.

1. Identify your goals. The first step in creating a plan for your money is to identify your goals. Every financial decision you make should be tested against your goals—how does a spending decision help or hinder your goal? The distribution of your income should reflect the commitment and priority you've placed on your goals. An acronym for defining goals is S-M-A-R-T. Each goal you want to achieve should be:

Specific – Be specific about what you want to accomplish. It's not enough to say that you want to save for a down payment for your home or pay off your debt. How *much* do you want to save or pay?

Measurable – How will you measure your progress? Have you designated a specific amount to save each month?

Achievable or attainable – the goal must be reasonable enough to ensure success and slightly uncomfortable so that you stretch yourself. To get something different, you must *do* something different.

Relevant– The goal must be meaningful and worthwhile. What is the reason for the goal? Is it meaningful? Does it fit in with your values?

Time Restricted – There must be a deadline. Every goal must have a committed deadline. By what date do you want to have your home down payment?

EXAMPLE: My goal is to eliminate $20,000 worth of debt over the next two years so that I can save a down payment for my future home. To reach this goal, I am going to allocate $833 each month in my budget for my debt payments. I plan to make the last payment in March 2021.

2. Track and analyze your current spending. This exercise is very enlightening. When my son first entered the military, he was clueless as to how to manage his new stream of income, and he consistently ran out of money before the next payday. He had no idea where his money was going. As co-signer on his banking account, I was able to access his banking activity. Taking a deep breath, I looked at his account and saw where he'd been eating fast food two and three times a day. I printed out his statement and highlighted the fast food transactions. When I finished, 90% of the page was yellow. I took a picture of the page and texted it to him. He was in disbelief. The visual alone was enough for him to get a handle on this problem. His bank statement revealed that he was spending upwards of $600 each month on fast food!

As part of my one-on-one coaching sessions, I routinely assign this exercise to my clients. Those who complete it are astonished to learn how much they spend on daily runs for gourmet coffee and breakfast sandwiches. Many of those who changed their daily spending habits saved over $100 each month and now use that money to pay down their credit card debt or add to their emergency savings.

Completing this exercise and analyzing the results can be a game changer. Seeing the results on paper helps you realize how imperative it is that you start to do some things differently if you want your financial situation to improve. When tracking your spending, try to capture every dollar, whether you're purchasing chewing gum or a refrigerator, paying a bill, or giving someone cash. No matter how small the cost, capture it. At the end of the month, all spending you tracked will be grouped to make up the line items of your budget.

3. Assign a dollar amount to your budget line items. After completing Step 2 of the budget process, you should have a pretty accurate picture of where your money is going. From your list, add the items that fall under the same category and allocate the total to the appropriate line item. For example, if you had ten purchases of food that month, add them all and assign the total amount to your budget line item for food. See the sample zero-based budget spreadsheet on the next page.

4. Monitor your progress frequently. Updating your budget should be done at least monthly. You'll enter your actual expenses from the previous month. Note the line items where you exceeded your planned spending or where you came in under budget. These are your adjustment opportunities. For example, if your childcare rates increase, you may have to balance the budget by decreasing a line item allocation, such as entertainment, so that your net budget always equals zero. Once you've identified areas for adjustments, you'll enter your projected income and expenses for the upcoming month.

Sample Zero-Based Budget

SMITH BUDGET for JANUARY 2019		
Category	Projected	Actual
INCOME (take home)		
Income 1	2,500	2,500
Income 2	3,000	3,000
Income 3	500	500
TOTAL INCOME	**$6,000**	**$6,000**
EXPENSES		
Mortgage/Rent	1,600	1,600
Utilities	300	300
Groceries	500	500
Transportation	600	600
Cell Phone	125	125
Medical	200	200
Life Insurance	50	50
Debt	700	700
Savings	300	300
Giving	300	300
Clothing	325	375*
Entertainment	300	300
Eating Out	250	300*
Discretionary Spending	450	450
TOTAL EXPENSES	**$6,000**	**$6,100**
DIFFERENCE		**(100)**

*The Smiths exceed their budget in two categories. They need to adjust their projections next month to make up for the overage. Each month's projected income and expenses must net to zero.

Budgeting Notes:

1. In a zero-based budget, every dollar of income must be assigned. The net of income and expenses must be zero.

2. If you're over or under budget in a category, adjust your projection for the following month. It will take a few months to get the budget stable.

3. If you have expenses that are paid on a cycle other than monthly, calculate the monthly budget by allocating 1/12th of the annual expense to each month.

4. Use the free budgeting app EveryDollar at everydollar.com. This app takes only ten minutes to set up, is super friendly, and provides spend tracking and budgeting tools. Best of all, it's internet-based, so you can access your budget any time on your laptop or mobile device. Before you begin using the app, draft your budget on a spreadsheet. This will help you enter your data quickly and ensure that you capture everything. If you prefer to use a spreadsheet for budgeting, you can download a pre-formatted spreadsheet at **zerobasedbudgethq.com**.[5] Edit the budget line items to personalize the spreadsheet.

It may take a few months to get your budget more exact. Be patient with yourself. If you become frustrated, focus on your goals and remind yourself that your efforts will pay off. Do not expect to get this right on the first or second try. You've developed your spending pattern over the years, and it will take time to change your habits. Your budget is a living document and will change as your financial status changes. Your income may change, as well as your goals. For example, as you pay off debt, you'll want to allocate those newly freed up funds to another line item in your budget. You'll need to adjust your budget for these events.

Coming up with a budget and maintaining a family financial plan should not be a spectator sport and everyone in the household bears some level of responsibility to do their part to ensure that the family meets its shared goals. The goals must be communicated and agreed upon. The best way to accomplish this is to have monthly family meetings to discuss your budget and make any adjustments necessary to meet your goals. The family's financial planning does not belong to the spouse who brings in the most income. They shouldn't get to make all the decisions without considering input from other members of the family.

Living your best life means you are aware of the feelings and needs of your loved ones, that you value their opinions, and you always put their best interest at heart when planning your finances. As spouses, you are no longer two, but one. And that means your resources are one, your goals are shared, and you hold each other accountable for sticking to the plan you created together. Most studies on marriage and divorce report that the discord over money and lack of communication are in the top three reasons for divorce. It is imperative that you talk through your concerns and come to a resolution that works for everyone—even if it means you both give in a little. If you fail or succeed, you do it together.

An essential part of family financial planning involves preparing for the day when one of you is no longer here. Unfortunately, many couples do not consider how drastically their life may change when their spouse dies. We don't like to talk about these things but dying is part of life and should be included in your financial planning. If you have anyone who is financially dependent on you, life insurance is a must. The primary purpose of life insurance is to ensure that your loved ones can continue to have their needs met and live the lifestyle you planned for them.

There is no shortage of stories of individuals dying without a life insurance, leaving their family financially destitute. I was traveling on an airplane and working on my laptop writing my book, *Money*

Management Wisdom for Millennials. The lady sitting next to me struck up a conversation. We talked about our grandkids, she has two and I had one at the time. She told me her daughter and grandkids lived with her. She didn't mention the circumstances as to why they were living with her. Being a long-distance grandma, I remember thinking how blessed she was to be able to see her grandchildren any time she wanted. She asked me what I was working on and I shared information about my book. I told her I was debating if I should include a section on life insurance being that my target audience is young adults who typically don't purchase life insurance. That's when she shared her story with me.

Her daughter was 24 years old when she married. Within four years, the couple had purchased a home and had two children. The lady said that she'd mentioned to her daughter and son-in-law several times that they needed to buy life insurance, but the young couple kept procrastinating. Unfortunately, her son-in-law was diagnosed with a terminal illness and no one would sell them an insurance policy they could afford. He eventually died having no life insurance. The daughter to sell their home because she could no longer afford the mortgage payments. The only life insurance policy was the small policy offered through the husband's employer which was barely enough to cover the funeral services and a few debts. Who knows what kind of financial future is in store for this family?

God forbid you should die and without having provided for your loved ones who are dependent on your financial support. Your children should not have to give up their dream of college or be forced to get into the student loan trap. Your family should not be forced to move out of their home because they can no longer afford the mortgage. And no one should have to start a Go Fund Me page to collect money to cover your end-of-life expenses or care for your family. Life for your family goes on, and their dreams are still alive. One of the most selfless, loving things you can do is to give your grieving family a measure of comfort in knowing that you loved them enough to make sure their needs are met—even in your absence.

A survey revealed that the number one reason people don't buy life insurance is that they think it's too expensive.[38] In reality, a healthy 40-year old woman can buy a 30-year, $500,000 policy for about $533 annually. A man of the same age can buy the same policy for $687. Combined, that's still less than the annual cost of cable television. You can't afford to *not* purchase life insurance when you consider the cost of not having any at all.

To live your best life, you must have a plan for your life, a plan for your money, and a plan to take care of your family. The Bible advises us to keep track and monitor our resources so that we can be prepared and have provisions in the future.[39] Living your best life means living with the confidence and peace that comes with knowing that you are doing all you can to prepare, plan, and secure a healthy financial future for you and your loved ones.

Step 6 - Get a Plan

Step 7 - Learn Contentment

Keep your lives free from the love of money and be content with what you have.
(Hebrews 13:5)

There's a story about a lady who purchased a lovely home many years ago. The house brought her much joy. Over the years, however, she became less enchanted with the home. She complained about the lake in the back of the house because it attracted too many mosquitoes and prevented her from enjoying evenings on the patio. She complained about the large oak trees that caused her to rake leaves in the fall. She also complained about the five-mile drive to the local grocery store. She finally decided to put the home on the market. She called her best friend, who is a realtor, and convinced her to list the house for sale and to start looking for her a new home to buy.

Several weeks later, the realtor called her friend with good news—she'd found her the perfect home. She described the house as having a beautiful view of a lake that would provide a cooling breeze during the summer months. She told her there were big beautiful trees that would create the perfect shading for the dog days of summer. She also mentioned that the home was in an area that was incredibly quiet and private with very little car traffic. The lady became excited as her friend described what sounded like the ideal house.

The realtor told her friend that she'd e-mailed pictures of the property and wanted her to look at the photos. The lady rushed to her computer to view the images. She stared at them a bit confusingly. As she focused a little more, she realized the pictures she was viewing were those of her own home.

You see, the lady was already living in her dream home. However, instead of focusing on the beauty, benefits, and joy the home brought, she focused on what she perceived to be the downfalls.

No situation is ever going to be perfect. There will always be tradeoffs. If you want to upgrade to a beachside home, you're going to have to deal with sand on the floors. If you're going to drive a luxury car, you've got to be okay with the additional cost of maintenance. If you want to make your way up the corporate ladder, you've got to deal with late nights, early mornings, and corporate politics. And, if you're going to run your own business, you've got to be willing to assume all the risks and sacrifices that come with being your own boss.

I recently participated in a financial conference where I taught a class on debt management. At the end of my session, a young man came to me with questions on the snowball method of debt elimination. He informed me that he had just paid off his car and was paying off his last credit card. His reason for wanting to become debt free? He wanted to purchase his dream car—a BMW, Series 4.

I asked him if he's planning to pay cash for the car and he replied that he is not. I asked why he would want to get out of debt just to go back into debt. His response was that he's always wanted a BMW. I asked why. He paused and shrugged his shoulders and responded, "I don't know; it's just been a dream." I asked if he had a car and if it was in good condition. He answered that the car he has is working great. So, I finally asked, "What is the BMW going to do for you that your current car cannot?"

I often use the method of asking a series of "why" questions when someone wants to purchase something they don't need or can't afford. After about the 3rd line of questioning, the person catches on. I know when they "get it" because they pause before answering and usually conclude that they really don't need to make the purchase, and that what they have is good enough. When we really get to the heart of the matter, many people are usually in pursuit of something to boost their image of how they want to be perceived by others.

People become dissatisfied with their current possessions and make it their life mission to seek the next thing that will make them happy. They are unable to live in the moment and opt to constantly pursue more, better, and best. The problem is that when they reach more, better, and best, they're still not satisfied. King Solomon said it best when he said that anyone who loves money (or the things that money can buy) is never satisfied, and anyone who loves wealth will never have enough income.[40]

To King Solomon's point, we can look at the scores of celebrities who have filed bankruptcy, were sentenced to jail for tax evasion, or committed tax fraud. They couldn't be content with the money and possessions they had, so they overspent, cheated, and lied about their money.

Apostle Paul, in his letter to his protégé, Timothy, claimed that the love of money is the root of all kinds of evil.[41] Some people, not being able to live a content life, find themselves doing all sorts of evil for the sake of money. The old school R & B group, the O'jays, echoed Paul's sentiment in the lyrics of their song, *For the Love of Money*:

For the love of money, people will steal from their mother
For the love of money, people will rob their own brother
For the love of money, people can't even walk the street
Because they never know who they're gonna meet
For that mean green

For the love of money, people will lie, rob, they will cheat
For the love of money, people don't care who they hurt or beat
For the love of money, a woman will sell her precious body
For a small piece of paper, it carries a lot of weight
For that mean green

As the song suggests, the love of money and the obsessive need for more can cause people to commit unscrupulous acts to fulfill their need for greed.

Living your best life is living a life of contentment. Contentment is merely knowing and trusting that whatever situation you're in, God has your back. It's having confidence that God knows your needs and desires. Contentment is understanding that as you walk in His will and your calling, nothing happens by chance. Everything that happens to you, good or bad, is divinely orchestrated to grow and shape you into the person He designed you to be. Whatever you have or don't have, if you're in His will, it is precisely what He wants for you at this moment.

Don't be confused. Contentment is not the same as complacency, neither does it mean that one should settle for whatever comes into their lives. You should make it a point to strive for improvements, advancements, and increase, but make sure you're doing so with the proper motives and that whatever you're seeking lines up with your calling.

Contentment is also not the same as being happy. Happiness is circumstantial. When things are going well, you're happy. But when things don't work out—you didn't get the promotion, your girlfriend or boyfriend breaks up with you, your flight was cancelled, or your request for a business loan was denied again— these circumstances make you unhappy. As Paul described in Philippians, contentment is not contingent upon an if-or-then situation. Contentment is constant regardless of what's going on around you. Contentment and joy reside in the same family—both are based on what you know to be true and are rooted in faith.

God doesn't ask us to accept what we perceive to be bad situations, but He does want us to *learn* to be content in them— meaning we're not going to complain about them to anyone who will listen, and we're not going to cry woe is me. We're going to be grateful that it isn't as bad as it could be. We're going to do what we can do to make the situation better. And, we're going to trust God while He works things out for our good—this is what practicing contentment looks like.

You might ask if being content seems so simple, why are so many people *not* content with their lives? One reason is that they constantly compare themselves to others. I mentioned the term comparative influence in Step Three as one of the barriers to financial wellness. The reason it's a barrier is that when we compare what we have to others, we develop a sense that we are somehow lacking. Without much thought or planning, we pursue those things we "lack" to the detriment of our financial health. We buy too much house, too much car, and too many clothes—not because we need them, but because we're trying to keep up with our friends or make a good impression. This need to create and maintain a certain image of how we want others to see us brings discontentment and causes us to become stressed, depressed, greedy, and broke.

Because of discontentment, individuals seek fulfillment in all the wrong places searching for that thing or person that will make their lives complete. They tell themselves that if they can just get that perfect house, car, man or woman, or a job making six figures, they can finally start living their best life.

Living your best life means being content when you want to buy a home or start a business, but your insufficient savings account and your low credit score are saying, "You've *got* to be kidding me." Does that mean you quit on your dream? No. That would be complacency, settling, and acceptance. If owning a home or starting a business is your goal, then you must do the work necessary to put you in a better financial position to acquire those things. Contentment says, "I'm not going to act irrationally, but I'm going to trust God to lead me through the process." If you take matters in your own hands to try to make things happen before God's time, it usually makes a tough situation worse, and you may not learn the lessons that come from patiently working through the process.

There is a favorite scripture often quoted by those who are trying to accomplish something big. Many people have the scripture tattooed on their body or printed on their attire. Philippians 4:13 says, "I can do all things through Christ who strengthens me." This verse can apply to anyone desiring to accomplish a challenging task. However, when taken in context, Paul was specifically referring to being content. Verse 11 says that Paul "learned" to be content through times when he had plenty and times when he was in need, times when he was hungry and times when he was well fed. His secret for getting through all those situations was to be content. In verse 13, he adds that he was only able to be content because of God's help (paraphrased).

So, where do you start learning contentment? It begins with being grateful. Be grateful for what you have, whether it's a little or a lot. Hebrews 13:5 tells us to keep our lives free from the love of money and to be content with what we have. When we express genuine appreciation for what we have, we don't focus on the things we don't have. Contentment is about learning to live faithfully *in the moment.*

You also learn to be content by trusting God. The second part of Hebrews 13: 5 continues saying that God will never leave us nor forsake us. In other words, He won't leave us hanging. When we trust God's promises and know that He wants the best for us, we can be confident that our prayers and desires are at the forefront of his mind. He loves us and wants us to be happy as we live in contentment waiting patiently for Him to take us to the next level— whatever that might look like.

Step 8 - Give Generously

Command them to do good, to be rich in good deeds, and to be generous and willing to share... *(1 Timothy 6:18)*

In a world where *getting* seems to be the primary purpose of existence for many people, it may be difficult to understand how giving is a significant part of the equation for living your best life. Everywhere you look, people are "out to get theirs," and often at the expense of others. Our selfishness tells us that to survive or become successful, we must think of ourselves first, and if there's anything left over, we might give or loan it to someone else. Giving to someone else means there is less for us.

On the other hand, there are people who consistently and willingly give their all. Whether it's time or money, they don't hesitate to meet the needs of others. They have a spirit of generosity that sometimes makes them a target for those inclined to take advantage of people's kindness.

Where is the happy medium on the giving scale? Who sets the standard? How can you live your best life through giving? To begin answering those questions, you must first understand the importance of having an attitude of gratitude. In Step One, you learned how to live your best life through stewardship by recognizing that everything you possess comes from God and that you are merely managers entrusted to oversee His blessings. You've acquired nothing through your own power. All things and any success you have is because God gave you the strength and endurance to accomplish it.[42]

Take a moment to pause and think about this. God has allowed you to have a place to live, food, transportation, a means of income, a good measure of health, and on and on. Not to mention the things he's spared you *from.* How many times have you seen terrible accidents on the highway or watched the news to see people who've lost everything to natural disasters? How often have you listened to reports of numerous lives lost to mass shootings? Countless mothers and fathers have lost their sons and daughters to violence, particularly gun violence. People are dying from car accidents and diseases—and yet, here you are.

The favor of God does not show itself only through material gain. He often shows His favor by withholding misfortune and providing protection from harm. Just watching the news will make you realize how blessed you are. If the realization of God's grace in your life does not affect you, it's time to check your spiritual pulse.

The heart is where your attitude of giving is born. The reason so many people find it difficult to give up their money or possessions to help others is that they have not had a change in their heart. You must remove selfishness, self-reliance, and entitlement from your heart and replace it with an attitude of gratitude. It is from the realization of the depth of God's grace in your life that giving becomes a privilege and an act of worship and thanksgiving.

In the Bible, Jesus and his disciples were ending a long tiring day when they received news that John the Baptist had been killed. Jesus decided to retreat to a remote place to be alone and pray. Before he could get away, a large crowd approached him with varying needs. Jesus' disciples admonished Him because it was getting late. The disciples suggested to Jesus that he send the crowd away to buy food for themselves. Instead, Jesus told the disciples to feed the crowd. Can you imagine what they were thinking? *"Here it is late in the evening. We've been supporting him all day while he taught and healed folks. We're tired, grieving, and ready to settle down for the night and he wants us to figure out the logistics of how to feed all these people? Is he kidding?"* But Jesus, unphased by the size of the crowd, blessed a young boy's lunch—two fish and five loaves of bread—multiplying it so that everyone had enough to eat. And there were leftovers.[43]

There are two kinds of hearts illustrated in this story. There's the passive heart and the active heart. The passive heart recognizes a need but stops short of actually meeting the need. The disciples were sensitive to the crowd's needs by acknowledging their hunger. However, instead of thinking how they could meet the crowd's need, their first thought was to send them away. On the other hand, Jesus felt compassion for the crowd, and it drove him to *do* something to address the problem. Jesus displayed an active heart. When we're operating in the spirit of giving, we need to give from a compassionate, active heart. "Thoughts and prayers" are lovely sentiments, but our giving should not stop there.

How often have we been privy to someone experiencing hardship with their finances, or someone who needs a job or a place to stay? Or, what about the mom in the checkout who doesn't have enough money to pay for her groceries? How often do we ignore the calls of church leaders for assistance in various ministries? As business owners, how often do we meet people who clearly need the service or product we sell but can't afford them? We see the needs, we *feel* their pain, but we stop short of providing when it is in our power to do so. We exercise our faith when we give to others.[44]

We need a grace reality check and an active heart. When you have a giving heart, you're not discriminate in what you choose to give. You'll give in the area where there is a need using the resources you have. God knows how much value we place on money and it makes sense that this is the area where he tests our heart condition.

We are all expected to be givers. Your level of income doesn't matter. Giving is the key to your greatest blessings. I've heard the act of giving explained like this: imagine a cup of water filled to the rim. The water represents your blessings—health, cars, house, clothes, your successful business, peace of mind, money, etc. You can pour your blessings out and waste them on meaningless, selfish endeavors and material things. Or, you can pour your blessings out to help others from your abundance and allow God to refill your glass with more blessings.

Where and how do you begin to give? Are there any rules or guidelines? I'm glad you asked. There are three categories from which you practice the act of giving. You can give of your financial resources, your time, and your skills and abilities.

The basis or rules for giving can be summed up in my favorite faith-based principle on giving, 2 Corinthians 9: 6-13. This passage summarizes the entire concept of giving:

"The point is this: whoever sows sparingly will also reap sparingly, and whoever sows bountifully will also reap bountifully. Each one must give as he has decided in his heart not reluctantly or under compulsion, for God loves a cheerful giver. And God is able to make all grace abound to you so that having all sufficiency in all things at all times, you may abound in every good work. As it is written, "He has distributed freely, he has given to the poor; his righteousness endures forever."

He who supplies seed to the sower and bread for food will supply and multiply your seed for sowing and increase the harvest of your righteousness. **You will be enriched in every way to be generous in every way** (my emphasis), *which through us will produce thanksgiving to God. For the ministry of this service is not only supplying the needs of the saints but is also overflowing in many thanksgivings to God. By their approval of this service, they will glorify God because of your submission that comes from your confession of the gospel of Christ, and the generosity of your contribution for them and for all others."*

What does this mean for you and how can you live your best life applying these principles?

You've probably heard the saying, "You reap what you sow." Sowing is the act of planting or putting something out in the universe as some would say. Reaping is the act of gathering or getting the results of what you planted. Some people call this karma. When it comes to giving, if you are stingy and miserly with your time, talents, and money, your blessings will flow to you in the same manner. Think of the glass of water. If you're already full because you don't give anything away, there is no room for you to get more.

Someone may need you to spend time listening to them or providing encouragement and counsel, but if you brush or rush them off, you may find that your time is "stolen" from you. Have you ever been spinning your wheels wishing you had more hours in the day? Where has your time gone? Did you invest your time in others? You may think you don't have time to give to anyone because you're already stretched. However, when you purposefully give time to others, it forces you to rethink your priorities and practice better time management.

It works the same way with money. You may think you're doing okay. You're able to pay your bills, you have a little money in the bank, and you're able to buy most of what you want. Imagine if you released some of your money to meet the needs of others. The passage above says, *"He who supplies seed to the sower and bread for food (God), will also increase the harvest of your righteousness."* In other words, when you give, it is God's job to reestablish your resources so that you never run out and your harvest (those who are the beneficiaries of your generosity) continues to grow and multiply (prosper and have their needs met). Isn't that amazing? It's as simple as understanding that the more you give, the more you get. Why? So that others can see the greatness of God through your generosity. You are blessed to be a blessing!

What are the guidelines for giving? The test to determine if you are on the right track for giving is to ask yourself three questions:

1. Are you giving willingly? Giving should be done out of your own free willingness to do so. Apostle Paul says that giving should not be done reluctantly or begrudgingly. Imagine someone giving you money or helping you with a project and complaining the entire time. How would that make you feel?

2. Are you giving cheerfully? If you aren't excited about giving and approach giving as something you *have* to do as opposed to something you *get* to do, it's time to check your heart. People want to know that you *want* to help them. For many people, it's difficult to accept help. But it's easier to accept help when someone is approaching the situation in an authentically cheerful and eager manner.

My parents separated when I was 12 years old. My dad's job was walking distance from where I lived with my mom and siblings. Whenever we needed something, mainly money, one of us would have to walk to my dad's job to ask for it. I hated doing that. He's my dad, and I should have been able to freely ask for what I needed. However, I knew that before receiving what I'd ask for, I'd have to endure a long lecture about money, the lack of it, the other uses he had for it, etc. One of the worst feelings is to have someone give you something reluctantly.

If you're going to help someone, either you do it or you don't, but don't make them endure a lecture or listen to a bunch of excuses.

3. Are you giving generously and sacrificially? To live your best life, it's essential that you learn to be a generous giver. Remember, you reap what you sow in the same measure you sowed. Your manner of giving reflects your gratitude, your love for God, and your love for people.

In the Bible, Paul conducted a fundraiser for the poor believers in Jerusalem. He praised the surrounding churches who were also poor because "they gave as much as they were able, and even beyond their ability. Entirely on their own, they urgently pleaded with us for the privilege of sharing in this service ."[45] Not only did the poor churches give what they had, they stretched themselves to dig a little deeper and gave more. To top it off, they thanked Paul for the *privilege* of being able to give. This is what sacrificial giving looks like.

I recently saw a video on social media that showed someone giving a homeless man money. The homeless man was so excited that he ran to the discount store across the street and purchased a blanket and pillow among other things. As he was returning to the bench, he saw a younger man sitting there having a phone conversation. As the homeless man approached the bench, he could hear that the man on the phone was distraught because he didn't have money to pay for his daughter's medicine. The homeless man gathered his bag of new purchases, walked back to the discount store and returned the items he'd just purchased. He returned to the bench where the young man was sitting and gave him the cash so the man could buy his daughter's medicine. This is what sacrificial giving looks like.

Finally, I can't write on the wisdom of biblical giving and how it fits in with living your best life without talking about the principle of tithing. In the Christian faith, we are taught that God requires believers to give 10% of their income to help support the mission and ministries of their local church. The topic of tithing generates much debate among Christians.

Some of the most frequently asked questions concerning tithing are:

- Is tithing still required for New Testament believers?
- Am I robbing God if I don't tithe?
- Am I sinning if I don't tithe?

Based on my studies and my understanding, I'm going to explain what God requires of us as it relates to giving, to include giving to support the church. The first thing you should know is that tithing (giving 10% of your income to support the church's mission) is *not* a commandment given under the new testament of grace. However, Jesus did not explicitly do away with the *concept* of tithing. In fact, he endorsed tithing when he admonished the Pharisees for being hypocrites. The Pharisees adhered strictly to tithing but neglected to exercise the more important matters of justice, mercy, and faithfulness. Jesus told them they should practice these things *without* neglecting the tithes.[46]

Under grace, Paul gives specific guidelines for giving in 2 Corinthians 9:6-15, a passage we visited earlier in this section. The two verses I want to emphasize are verses six and seven. To paraphrase, we should purpose in our "hearts" (make up our mind) what we are going to give and then follow the guidelines of the entire passage as it relates to giving cheerfully, generously, and sacrificially. When we give in this manner, God promises to replenish our resources so that we can continue to be givers. When we become willing, cheerful, sacrificial givers, our reputation will become known to others and ultimately draw others to God— fulfilling our ultimate purpose.

So, what about 10%? I view the giving of 10% as a guideline, not a requirement, based on the standard set in the old testament. It is the minimum that we should work towards. Think of it as the training wheels of giving. I wish church leaders and teachers wouldn't place a great emphasis on the fixed number of 10% and here's why: those who are able and willing to give 10% may become comfortable that they've met the standard and thus become arrogant, complacent, and unwilling to do more because they have "arrived." Those who genuinely are not able to give 10% due to circumstances beyond their control may become discouraged, disappointed, and may even avoid giving altogether. If people are taught more about God's love, grace, mercy, and the benefits of being a generous giver, they will grow to become givers from a heart of gratitude for all that God provides—material or otherwise.

We can look to Zacchaeus as an example of giving from a grateful heart. Zacchaeus was a hated, ruthless tax collector who took advantage of his position to extort money from people on behalf of the Roman government. Zacchaeus was not just any tax collector, he was the *chief* tax collector which made him the most despised person. Then he met Jesus. Once Zacchaeus spent time with Jesus and realized that Jesus could love even him, his heart changed. Under the Mosaic law, people were required to give 10%, and in some cases, 23%. What does Zacchaeus do after his heart transplant? He promises to make restitution to the people he scammed *and* give away 50% of all he owned!

When people's hearts are changed, they won't need to be reminded of a standard. They need only to be mindful of God's grace and mercy and follow Paul's guidelines for giving. Their changed hearts will propel their giving above and beyond expectations. They will happily remove their training wheels and others will be witness to their generosity. Ron Blue, the author of *Never Enough*, puts it this way: "As God gets ahold of our hearts, it will be obvious to the world by our attitudes toward money. We will live lives that are free from fear, greed, envy, and materialism."[47] Our giving will become generous because our primary focus will not be on our own needs or desires—God's got that covered.

Know that your choice to tithe or not tithe has no bearing on your salvation. You're not going to heaven because you tithe and you're not going to hell if you don't. Under grace, you're not robbing God if you don't tithe. However, you may be depriving yourself of blessings if you're not following the guidelines of biblical giving. God wants to bless you abundantly with more than you can ever imagine,[48] but you must first empty your glass. Think about this: the people from the old testament had no grace, no mercy, no forgiveness, and no savior to die for their sins, yet they were required to give 10% or more. As Christians who have the benefits of God's grace, mercy, forgiveness, and sacrificial death, how do we justify giving anything less?

It doesn't matter if our resources are large or small, we're all called to be givers, not only from our financial resources but also giving of our time and skills. Decide what you want to give from your heart and be consistent. I promise, as your gratitude grows, so will your giving. God promised that when you give, you will be enriched in every way. In. Every. Way. This means your family and business will prosper, your needs will be met, and every area of your life will be blessed. When you learn to give the right way and with the right motives, you will truly be living your best life.

Final Thoughts

I hope you find this 8-Step journey to living your best life educational and inspiring and that you gain a new perspective on money. Everyone has the potential to live a life of purpose and to be fulfilled in whatever area they are called to serve. Money is an essential aspect of life, and our relationship with money can build us up or tear us apart. Money can bring us our greatest joys, and it can also be the cause of our biggest sorrows. Money is powerful in that it can be used to effect monumental change in people's lives—for good or bad.

If you're struggling to put your financial life in order, know that your situation is not hopeless. Reading this book shows that you are ready to take steps towards a better financial future and a better life. I've found that in most cases where individuals follow a well-crafted, concrete plan that includes goals and is based on biblical principles, they start to see significant improvements in their life.

I can attest that managing your money the right way pays off. If you're willing to make sacrifices, it will be well worth it. My husband and I became 100% debt free in October 2018 when we paid off our 15-year mortgage in eight years. We have no credit card balances or car payments. We don't owe anyone a dime. But it didn't happen overnight. It was a journey of intentionality. Now, we can bump up our retirement savings, spoil our grandkids, and give more to those in need, and it feels wonderful. Visit my website, moneymanagementwisdom.net and read the blog, *Seven Dollars Changed my Life*, which is the story of when and how I developed my perspective of money. I was a teenager when I had my epiphany. What will it take for you to begin to see things differently?

This is a journey you've decided to take for the betterment of you and your family. Many of your friends and family may not understand your new direction or the sacrifices you'll start to make.

You may be tempted to continue doing some of the things that likely put you in a negative financial situation. When it gets tough, remember your goals, your calling, and your purpose. Stay focused on your desired outcomes and make decisions that will most likely give you the results you want.

As you walk through these eight steps, think about your legacy. What values do you want to pass along to those coming behind you? What stories will your children and grandchildren tell about you? It's not so much about the material inheritance you leave for the next generations. What's more important is the inheritance of good values, a generous spirit, and a passion for helping others.

My prayer for you is that you understand the great responsibility you have to yourself, your family, and your creator to manage your money in a way that helps you and future generations live in prosperity in every area of your lives.

Discussion Questions

1. Are you aware of your unique role or calling in life? If so, how does your current financial situation affect your calling?

2. In what ways have you practiced good stewardship? What area (s) do you find most challenging? (Refer to Page 15.)

3. Which of the four barriers to financial wellness—lack of self-control, lack of discipline, procrastination, or comparative influences—has had the most impact on your bottom line? How?

4. Step Four mentions that the average household carries more than $15,000 in credit card debt. Does this surprise you? Why or why not?

5. Statistics report that most people do not have an emergency fund. Why do you think building an emergency fund is not a top priority for most people?

6. In Step Six, you are encouraged to have a plan for your life and your money. Are you able to define your life's plan? If so, how does your financial behavior (spending, saving, and giving) reflect those plans?

7. What steps can you take to begin *learning* how to master contentment?

8. Three areas where we can become givers are time, talents (skills) and money. Which of these areas would be the easiest for you to apply the guidelines of willful, cheerful, generous, and sacrificial giving? Which would be the most challenging?

Also by Merrie Allmon Allen

Money Management Wisdom for Millennials

Available for workshops and speaking engagements.
To inquire, visit moneymanagementwisdom.net, or email
moneymanagementwisdom@gmail.com

NOTES

[1] Hosea 4:6

[2] Romans 12:2

[3] Ecclesiastes 12:13, I Corinthians 10:31

[4] Ephesians 2:10

[5] Valorie Burton, *Successful Women Think Differently*, (Oregon: Harvest House Publishing, 2012).

[6] Psalms 24:1

[7] Matthew 6:24-25

[8] Luke 16:10

[9] Matthew 25:14-30

[10] Jane Hunt, Financial Freedom: How to Manage your Money Wisely, Aspire Press, 2014, p29

[11] https://www.merriam-webster.com/dictionary/self-control

[12] https://www.verywellfamily.com/the-importance-of-teaching-children-impulse-control-1095019

[13] Galatians 5:22

[14] https://www.merriam-webster.com/dictionary/discipline

[15] https://www.merriam-webster.com/dictionary/procrastination

[16] Jane Hunt, *"Procrastination: Preventing the Decay of Delay,"* Aspire Press, 2015, p32

[17] https://countryeconomy.com/demography/life-expectancy/usa

[18] Ecclesiastes 11:4

[19] Proverbs 13:4 (NLT)

[20] Proverbs 13:7

[21] Psalms 139:14

[22] https://www.fool.com/credit-cards/2017/12/11/heres-the-average-american-households-credit-car-2.aspx

[23] https://www.cnbc.com/2018/07/19/consumers-paying-104-billion-in-credit-card-interest-and-fees.html

[24] https://www.creditcards.com/credit-card-news/cardholder-satisfaction-rewards-security-statistics-1276.php

[25] Ecclesiastes 4:4

[26] Proverbs 10:22

[27] Proverbs 6:1-5

[28] James 1:17

[29] https://studentloanhero.com/student-loan-debt-statistics/

30 https://www.payscale.com/research/US/Job=Elementary_School_Teacher/Salary

[31] Psalms 37:21

[32] https://www.cnbc.com/2017/09/13/how-much-americans-at-have-in-their-savings-accounts.html

[33] Ecclesiastes 11: 1-6

[34] https://www.statista.com/statistics/274513/life-expectancy-in-north-america/

[35] Exodus 32:15

[36] Habakkuk 2:2

[37] Luke 14:28-31

[38] https://www.nerdwallet.com/blog/insurance/average-life-insurance-rates/

[39] Proverbs 27:23-27

[40] Ecclesiastes 5:10

[41] 1 Timothy 6:10

[42] Deuteronomy 8:18

[43] Matthew 14:13-21

[44] James 2:14-17

[45] 2 Corinthians 8:3-4

[46] Matthew 23:23-24

[47] Ron Blue, Never Enough, Nashville, TN, B & H Publishing, 2017

[48] Ephesians 3:20

www.ingramcontent.com/pod-product-compliance
Lightning Source LLC
Chambersburg PA
CBHW060626210326
41520CB00010B/1483